P9-CCH-924

Magus of the Library

Mitsu Izumi

Based on *Kafna of the Wind*

Written by Sophie Schwimm • Translated by Hiroto Hamada

4

Magus of the Library 4

CHAPTER 15 The Continent is Small, Fly on Syrrana 5

CHAPTER 16 Blood Will Be Drawn When Nobles Draw Forth 55

CHAPTER 17 An Almost Transparent Future 123

CHAPTER 18 Acting the High and Mighty Regal Curatrix 159

CHAPTER19 Reunion at Aftzaak 201

"Entrenchment"
Scene from the performance art piece *The Legend of the Great Magus*

"No theft a crime if Haupi purse,
no trespass wrong if Haupi shamed,
no murder sin if Haupi blood."

—Zarama Ingare'i
From ***The Words of Justice***

Libraries...
...and monuments to all life across time.
...galleries dedicated to history's thread...
Amassers of memory...
To the people, it was known as the Great Central Library.
...one stood above the rest, directing all others.
And of those myriad amassers and galleries...

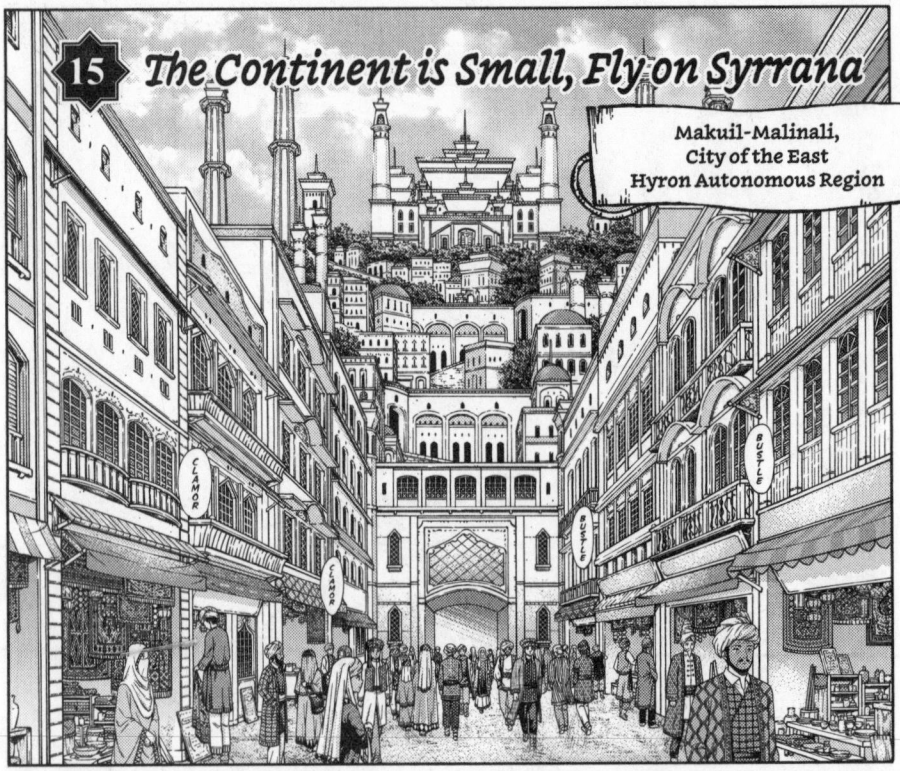

Hikinnawai, the Eastern Perch
Temple of the Asin Faith

In the religion of Asin...
Asin's followers were many among the Hyron, matched only in number by those devoted to Manaccha, the Way of Mana.
...there is but one god—Viracocha, the creator.

MURMUR
MURMUR
MURMUR
MURMUR
MURMUR
MURMUR
MURMUR...
MURMUR...
MURMUR
MURMUR
MURMUR
Eek! Get away!
HEY! YOU SEEIN' THIS?!
WHAT'S A DIRTY RAKTA DOIN' WALKIN' AROUND?
Run him outta town!
Think he's a spy?!
Look at that smug face!

AHAHAHAHA!
GET LOST, SLANT-EYES!
THAK
KAFWAP
?!
I CAN'T HELP IT! IT'S SO FUN SEEING THE REALLY DEVOUT BELIEVERS REACT TO OUTSIDERS.
Weirdo.
Ah ha ha!
DID I NOT MAKE MYSELF CLEAR? YOU ARE HERE AS A KAFNA, SO DRESS AS ONE. AT ALL TIMES.
ERP!
ARE THEY ...?!
KRNCH
KRNCH
KRNCH
KRNCH
KRNCH
UH-OH! SOMEONE'S IN TROUBLE AGAIN!

KRNCH

RESTRAIN YOURSELF, MAGUS.
YOUR SERVICES SHALL NOT BE REQUIRED.
CENTRAL LIBRARY, LIAISONS OFFICE
AYLBA CANHEL
MAYBE I'LL FINALLY GET TO BREW UP A STORM!
CENTRAL LIBRARY, PROTECTIONS OFFICE
MAHUIA TETEO
SHALL WE HEAD ON IN, THEN?
CENTRAL LIBRARY, JUDICIAL OFFICE
KAZ BLAK
KRNCH
KRNCH
KRNCH
KRNCH
THE KAFNA ARE HERE!
IT'S THE KAFNA!
Makuil-Malinali Public Library
TO WHAT DO WE OWE THIS HONOR?
DEAR ME. HOW VERY UNEXPECTED.
CARETAKER
YOL CUATT

IT'S ALL FULLY AUTHORIZED. HERE. OUR WRIT OF INVESTIGATION.
YES, MA'AM!
TMP
LAY THEM OUT OVER THERE, PLEASE.
WE'RE CONDUCTING AN ON-SITE INVESTIGATION.
TMP
NOW SEE HERE...!
WHAT'S THE MEANING OF THIS?!
Shelving Bias
A violation of the Library Code, wherein certain books are intentionally made unavailable for consumption.
WE RECEIVED A COMPLAINT THAT THIS BRANCH MAY BE ENGAGED IN SHELVING BIAS.
AND OUR PRELIMINARY FINDINGS APPEARED TO SUPPORT THAT CLAIM.
By Central Library mandate, books are to be arranged according to certain rules.
For example, books upholding a given theory as true must be shelved in the same section as books denouncing that same belief.
Removing all books aligned with a dissenting position or arranging them in a manner that makes them difficult to find is strictly forbidden.
SHRF...

LEAN
MOVE ASIDE, FELLA! WE HAVE WORK TO DO!
ERP!
SHRF
?!
LOOM...
ARRIVING HERE WITHOUT NOTICE IS MOST DISRUPTIVE.
DEPART AT ONCE. YOU MAY PROCEED WITH THE INVESTIGATION TOMORROW.

I WANT A THOROUGH SEARCH OF THE CIRCULATION RECORDS! REPORT ANY FOUL PLAY!
AND FIND OUT WHETHER THE CATALOG MATCHES THE SHELVES!

SIR BLAKK, WE'VE FOUND SOMETHING.

THUMP
THUMP
WHUMP
EVEN IF THEY'RE ON THE SHELVES, WE STILL NEED TO CHECK THEM OVER. LOOK FOR MISSING PAGES! BLACKENED PASSAGES!

BEGIN WITH TITLES WE OUTLINED BEFORE-HAND.

Clip-ping
A violation of the Library Code, wherein the names of individuals who check out certain books are recorded and indexed.
IT APPEARS TO IDENTIFY THOSE CHECKING OUT BOOKS BY WRITERS CRITICAL OF ASIN.
WE'VE GOT OURSELVES A CLIP LIST. Well done!
NOW IT'S JUST A QUESTION OF WHO THEY'VE BEEN SHARING THIS WITH.
MY, MY.
KRACKLE
YIPE!
KREEK...
...
NURNUR
NURNUR
SHELF TWO IS DONE!
BUSTLE
BUSTLE
HOLD IT RIGHT THERE!
KLUNK
DON'T TRY ANYTHING SNEAKY, OR YOU'LL BE IN FOR A SHOCK.
BZZT
BZZT
BZZT
BZZT
KSH
FWSH

BLAST!
DONATION RECORDS.
...
RUSTLE...
THESE ARE--
ANY CLUE WHICH ORGANIZATION MIGHT BE BEHIND THIS?
COULDN'T SAY. THE POSSIBILITIES ARE ENDLESS.
AND A NUMBER OF THE BENEFACTORS GO UNNAMED.
LOOKS LIKE WE KNOW WHERE TO START PRYING.
BUT IT MATTERS NOT. FREEDOM OF CHOICE IS ABSOLUTE.
THE LIBRARY WILL NOT TOLERATE ANYONE WHO INFRINGES UPON IT, NO MATTER WHO THEY ARE.
FWSH
FWSH

CON-FOUND IT ALL...
MEDDLE-SOME KAFNA!

Throughout time, the powerful have desired that commoners stay ignorant so that they may be more easily exploited in military recruitment and the collection of taxes.
Despots knew a single spark could be enough to incite the populace's anger and quickly topple their regimes.

Information and control have always gone hand in hand.

At times, texts were altered. At times, they were burned. Many were the schemes to keep knowledge from the people's grasp, and so fruitful were they...
KRNCH
And in any effort to suppress the flow of information, control over the written word is key.
...it was said that whoever had control of the land's texts held the reins of the continent itself.
Based on Kafna of the Wind
KRNCH
KRNCH

KRNCH
KRNCH
In the words of a certain magus...
KRNCH
KRNCH
KRNCH

"To protect a text...
...is to protect...
...the world itself."
by Sophie Shwimm
KRNCH

突撃前

書の大
Magus of the Library

Library
4

Magus of the

Part 2

"Days in Training at the Central Library"

ENJOYING THE RIDE BACK THERE?
WRRSH
VSSHHH
YOWII
OF THE SYRRANA
YES! IT'S VERY COMFORTABLE, MISS YOWII!
There is a line of thought...
TO THE SYRRANA, THE WHOLE CONTINENT IS BUT A BACKYARD RETREAT.
HEE HEE...
WINGS SURE ARE AMAZING!
IT TOOK ME DAYS TO CROSS THIS MOUNTAIN RANGE, BUT NOW WE'RE SOARING RIGHT BY.

...set forth by the Great Thinker Zarud, known as the "Origin of Tharms."
The theory holds that the many varied races peopling the continent today derive from a single, small creature that lived long ago.
A lobino, the creature posited by Zarud to be the ancestor of all humanoid races.

Legend holds that the Syrrana have resided on the continent since the distant past—long before the appearance of other civilizations.
The Syrrana, however, are thought to be wholly unrelated.
THE CAVE DRAWINGS OF GRICKOIRE

In Tawals' epic novel Legend of the Great Hero, mankind receives the gift of knowledge from a dragon. That creature is thought to have been modeled after the Syrrana people.
I KINDA LIKE THAT STORY OF HOW THINGS CAME TO BE. IT SOUNDS SO EXCITING.

ARE WE NOT HEADED TO AFTZAAK?
MY, MY...
YOU'RE QUITE PERCEPTIVE, AREN'T YOU?

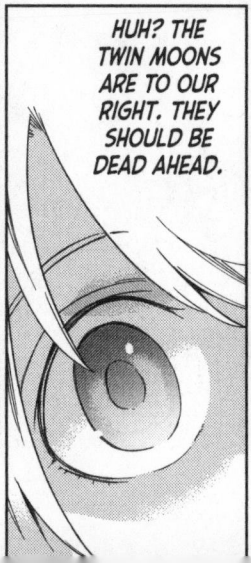
HUH? THE TWIN MOONS ARE TO OUR RIGHT. THEY SHOULD BE DEAD AHEAD.

A GOOD FRIEND OF MINE ASKED THAT WE SHOW YOU THE SIGHTS.
SIGHTS?
!!
WHIRL
EEP!
OBSERVE.
'TIS THE ASHEN WORLD BELOW US NOW.

SHIVER...
THESE ARE THE SCARS WROUGHT BY THE EMISSARY OF WORMWOOD, STILL SHROUDING SO MUCH OF THE CONTINENT TODAY...
THE ASHEN DEATH...
NUMEROUS DELEGATIONS JOURNEY TO THE FRINGES TO SURVEY THE ASHEN WORLD.
...
DOES THAT MEAN THERE'S NO LIFE AT ALL DOWN THERE?
I'VE BEEN TAUGHT THAT PEOPLE CAN'T SURVIVE INSIDE THE FOG.
THRMP
YIP YIP!
THRR RMP
FLINCH
THEIR REPORTS TELL US THAT LIFE IS IN NO SHORT SUPPLY AMONG THE WHITE.
RMM BLL
KRNCH

THE SURVEY TEAMS REFER TO THEM AS THE DENIZENS OF THE ASH.
RMMBL

BUT IF WE'RE SOARING ABOVE THE FOG NOW, DOES THAT MEAN SYRRANA ARE ABLE TO JOURNEY BEYOND THE ASHEN WORLD?!
BUT OF COURSE.
BEFORE YOU ASK, THOUGH, KNOW THAT THESE EARS ARE DEAF TO ANY PLEAS TO SEE THE SEA.
The Denizens of the...
GULP ...
WAIT!
THIS IS A BURDEN BY THE OTHER RACES BORN AND BORNE.
IN MATTERS OF THE ASHEN WORLD, THE SYRRANA STAND FIRM. WE SHALL NOT LEND AID.
THE ASHEN DEATH
WE SHALL TAKE A SHORT TOUR OF THE NEARBY REGIONAL SEATS BEFORE HEADING INTO AFTZAAK.
NOW, LET US PROCEED TO OUR NEXT DESTINATION.
AMUN
KALAR
ITZAMNA
BULWARK OF OMEN
ESPLEO
LAKE TATA
BELEHEBEI-TZI
WHERE'S THAT?

BEFORE YOU LIES KALAR, CITY OF THE STARS—SEAT OF THE RAKTA AUTONOMOUS REGION.
KALAR...
THIS IS THE CITY OF A PEOPLE WHO ONCE HUGGED THE SEA, ONLY TO BE DRIVEN FROM THEIR HOMELANDS BY THE EMISSARY...
ONWARD.

NOW WE PASS THE BORDER BETWEEN HYRON AND RAKTA LANDS. THE STRUCTURE BELOW IS THE BULWARK OF OMEN.
IS THAT A SPIRIT ?!
WHAT IN THE BLAZES ?!
THANKS TO THE MANA DEPOSITS MINED NEARBY, THIS BOUNDARY IS EVER MIRED IN DISPUTE.
ONE MIGHT SAY THE WALL IS A SYMBOL OF THE GREAT WAR THAT HAS NEVER TRULY ENDED.
HEE HEE...
AND NEXT...

...WE ARRIVE AT BELEHEBEI-TZI, CITY OF THE FATHER. THIS IS THE SEAT OF THE HYRON.

THAT MUST BE MAOKAFHUA, THE GREEN PERCH.
THAT'S THE SEAT OF THE HYRON CENTRAL GOVERNMENT.

FWIRSH

AND AT LONG LAST...
AFTZAAK, THE CITY OF BOOKS.

WHUMP
WE'LL BE MAKING SOME ANNOUNCEMENTS SOON. ONCE YOU'VE SEEN TO YOUR BELONGINGS, COME TO THE READING SALON.
THOSE PACKS MUST MEAN THEY'RE BOTH ALREADY HERE!
WOW. ROOMMATES.
MANY OF THE OTHER TRAINEES HAVE ALREADY BEEN IN AFTZAAK FOR A FEW DAYS NOW.
THERE ARE TWO OTHER BOYS THIS YEAR. YOU'LL BE ROOMING TOGETHER.

THAT CAN WAIT.
I'VE GOT BIGGER WORRIES. SOON I'LL BE INTRODUCING MYSELF TO THE OTHER TRAINEES.
Holdin' down the fort!
HOW DO YOU DO?
HOW DO YOU DO?
WELL-HEELED CITY GIRLS ARE PROBABLY QUIET AND POLITE. ESPECIALLY ONES THAT DREAM OF BEING KAFNA.
PLEASED TO MEET YA!!
IS EVERYONE GONNA STICK TO THEIR OWN CUSTOMS?
NO! THERE'S NOTHING WRONG WITH A CONFIDENT, ENTHUSIASTIC GREETING!
SHAKE SHAKE SHAKE
I JUST GOTTA WALK TALL AND GIVE IT MY ALL, NO MATTER WHAT!
TMP
IS IT ME, OR DOES SOMETHING SMELL LIKE A FARM?
OH, MY. HE SURE IS LOUD.
How barbaric.
Grk...

PAUSE...
ゴク…ッ
GULP...

...!
...HERE GOES!
FFFT...
SPRING
PLEASED TO MEET...
TMP
TMP
TMP
...Y-
IT'S...!
THEOOOOO!!!
AAAH!
KMRPPH!
KAFWOMP
BOUND

MHGGA! MHTS MU!
NICE CATCH!
Mrmph!
YAY!
YAY!
OHGGA! WHAT A RELIEF! I'M SO HAPPY YOU PASSED!
HEY! YOU CUT YOUR HAIR! IT LOOKS GREAT!
THANKS! ALWAYS THE CHARMER!
WHASSUP!
I GET TO BECOME A KAFNA ALONGSIDE YOU?! I CAN'T THINK OF ANYTHING BETTER!
NATICA'S HERE, TOO, Y'KNOW?
SHE IS?!
DIANASYS DI'OHGGA

HMPH. SO WEUWEU MADE THE CUT, TOO.
Tsk!
WHEN I TRIED TO GIVE HER A HUG, I GOT A SLAP ACROSS THE CHEEK.
...
I'M SURE SHE WAS JUST TRYING TO FOCUS ON HER READING.
NATICA QUAPAN
'COURSE, NATICA'S NOT THE ONLY ONE. EVERYONE HERE IS TRYING TO FEEL THINGS OUT.
REALLY?
NAH, SHE HASN'T READ A SINGLE WORD OF THAT THING.
MISS SHIFTY EYES HAS BEEN SCOPING OUT THE ROOM THIS ENTIRE TIME.
GRK! THAT BLASTED HUONE!
How'd she know?!
SURE! AND FROM THEIR GAZES, I CAN TELL THEY'VE GOT THEIR EYES ON ME.
I MEAN, I IMAGINE IT'S HARD NOT TO STARE...
BY THE WAY...

IT LOOKS LIKE SOMEONE ELSE WANTS TO SAY HI.
HM?
EEEP!
AHHH!
HOW RUDE OF ME! I'M SO SORR--
HUH?! MISS SOHN?!
I CANNOT EXPRESS HOW DELIGHTED I AM...
...FOR US TO...
...THAT WE MIGHT...
WOW! THAT'S GREAT! YOU PASSED, TOO!
HEY, I REMEMBER YOU FROM THE PRACTICAL EXAM!
PLEASE ACCEPT MY HUMBLE APOLOGIES. I WAS NOT SURE WHEN BEST TO APPROACH YOU.
SALA SEI SOHN
BLUSH
...HAVE THIS... OPPORTUNITY TO REUNITE...!

I'M HERE! I'M REALLY HERE FOR REAL!
THIS IS THE BUILDING WHERE ALL NEW KAFNA BEGIN THEIR STUDIES!
HEY THERE, THEO!
I KNEW YOU'D PASS. YOU WERE A SHOO-IN!
I'M SO GLAD TO SEE YOU AGAIN!
WHOA!
It gets this sprite feelin' real sprightly!
HUH?! HEY!
PEPERICO?!
PEPERICO PRADHATTI
GEE GOLLY, JUST THINKING ABOUT HOW I GET TO WITNESS ALL YOU TRAINEES SPREADING YOUR WINGS AND TAKING TO THE SKIES AS KAFNA...
UM, I'M PRETTY SURE YOU'RE GONNA BE TRAINING RIGHT THERE WITH US...
IT GETS MY HEART A-THUMPIN'!
I GOTTA GET CRACKIN'! I'LL START WITH THE KIDS STANDIN' ON THEIR OWN.
I'LL BE BACK TO GET THE DEETS FROM YOU AND YOUR FRIENDS LATER, THEO!
SHE'S, UH... REALLY INTO KAFNA, YOU SEE?
?
...
LOOKS LIKE THE OTHERS HAVE ALREADY BEGUN TO ASSEMBLE. I SUPPOSE WE OUGHT TO HEAD DOWN, TOO.

SO YOU GREW UP NEAR BOOK-SELLERS' ROW?
WOW. I'VE ALWAYS DREAMED OF VISITING ITZAMNA.
PLEASE DO! IT WOULD BE MY PLEASURE TO SHOW YOU AROUND.
Hehe...
KA-CHAK
MIHONA QOAHAU
LOOKIN' SUAVE, MIHONA.
THINGS ARE GOING GREAT.
YOU'RE ON TRACK FOR AN IMPECCABLE FIRST IMPRESSION.
NOBODY HERE KNOWS THE FIRST THING ABOUT MY PAST!
I'M STARTING OUT ON THE RIGHT FOOT FOR A DAZZLING KAFNA DEBUT!!
OH, HEY!
HOW'S IT GOING, MIHO–
FWOING
NGRK!!

WAS THAT A FRIEND OF YOURS?
SEEMS LIKE HE GOT THE WRONG PERSON.
You got this!
WHIRL
?!
Ngrk?
!!
THANKS, THEO.
YOU'RE A STANDUP GUY.
JUST WATCH AS I CRAFT A SLEEK, STYLISH IDENTITY FOR THIS NEW CHAPTER OF MY LIFE!
I WON'T WASTE THIS CHANCE YOU'VE GIVEN ME.
SNAG
ACK !!
KERPLUMP

KRNCH
MAKING A SCENE LIKE ALWAYS, ISN'T SHE?
!
I GOTTA ADMIT, I NEVER EXPECTED THE TWO OF YOU TO PASS.
Oh, no! Poor Minona!
Are you hurt?!
FWOING
THAT'S GR-
!
...!
WHAT'S THE MATTER?
HEH!
You seem outta breath.
I GUESS THE TRAINEE'S EXAM IS EASIER THAN EVERYONE THINKS.
HFF... HFF...
ALV! YOU'RE HERE, TOO!
ALV TLALOQUE
SKE
DADDLE
SORRY, BLONDIE. GOTTA RUN.
KEEP HIM BUSY FOR ME, WILL YA?

OH
HE'S EXCITABLE, BUT GIVE HIM A GOOD WHACK AND HE'LL SETTLE DOWN!
BOY
OH
HIM WHO?
BOY
OH
BO OOOY!!
KAFWAMP
IT'S TRUE ...!
THERE IS ANOTHER BOY HERE!! NOT JUST ONE, BUT TWO!!
WH...
THANK THE MAGUS!
OHHH ...
WHAT'S GOING ON?!

OHHH BOYYY!
IT'S JUST... THREE BOYS IN THE SAME CLASS! I'M SO HAPPY!
SORRY... FORGIVE ME...
SUMOMO KAVISHMAF
FLOMP
DO YOU KNOW WHAT THIS IS?!
IT'S FATE! FATE, I TELL YOU!
I WAS SO SCARED THAT I'D BE ALONE HERE!
AND I WAS THE ONLY BOY TO PASS!
YOU WOULDN'T BELIEVE HOW OUT-NUMBERED WE WERE AT PREP SCHOOL!
THEY NEVER LEFT US BOYS ALONE!!
HEH, HEH, HEH... LOOK AT THEM ALL. A REAL BATCH OF WEIRDOS.
...
UGH. I GOTTA SPEND THE NEXT YEAR WITH THAT GUY?
IT'S AN HONOR TO MEET YOU, THEO!
ERM... YEAH! YOU, TOO!

HEY, IT'S NOT AN INSULT. I'M JUST SAYING LIFE AROUND HERE IS GONNA BE INTERESTING.
I WOULD VENTURE THAT YOU ARE THE *LAST* PERSON TO BE DESCRIBING OTHERS AS STRANGE.
I CAN ASSURE YOU, I WILL BE FINE.
YOU NEEDN'T CODDLE ME, KANA.
AYA GUUNJOH
'COURSE, I *AM* A LITTLE WORRIED WHETHER YOU'LL MANAGE TO MAKE ANY NEW FRIENDS.
KANA MIDOREEN

* ATLATONAN: THE GREAT SPIRIT SAID TO HAVE FORMED THE CONTINENT ITSELF

EXCUSE ME?!
?!
YOU WANNA SAY THAT AGAIN?!
HAVE YOUR EARS FAILED YOU?
I *TOLD* YOU TO LEAVE ME BE. PEASANTS SHOULD KNOW BETTER THAN TO PESTER THOSE OF PROPER BIRTH.
C'MON, MADHA. DON'T MAKE A SCENE...
I WAS *TRYIN'* TO GIVE THIS GIRL A COMPLIMENT! ALL I SAID WAS THAT HER BIRD IS PRETTY SWEET.
DON'T TALK TO YOU, HUH?! WELL, EAT THIS!
WHAT'S YER NAME?!
WHERE YA FROM ?!
WHAT KINDA STUFF' ARE YA INTO?!
MADHA! ENOUGH!

SHING
ZRSH
PERHAPS YOUR FAILURE TO LISTEN REFLECTS A FAILURE TO UNDERSTAND. ALLOW ME TO INSTRUCT YOU.

The Kafna in Training
The Banded Few
Theo Fumis
A boy of Hyron and Haupi heritage. Though raised in the slums, he balanced a life of study and work and managed to pass the kafna exam. His greatest strengths are his stamina and physical constitution, honed over years of labor at Ganan Masonry.
Sumomo Kavishmaf
A Hydiah boy hailing from a large and respected house known for producing many kafna. His guileless demeanor is marred only by the occasional consequent lapse in etiquette. Skittish around girls and women thanks to the many overbearing personalities surrounding him as he grew up.
Alv Tlaloque
A boy of rather small stature. Pretends not to care about his height, yet dreams of a long-awaited growth spurt. Had the second-highest exam score of this incoming class. Actually quite gifted at navigating social situations when he chooses, and thus completed the exam's practical component with ease.

The Kafna in Training
The Seaborn Souls
Kana Midoreen
A Rakta girl and longtime friend of Aya's. At 172 cm, she stands tallest among this class of trainees. Requires little sleep and is thus exceptionally well-read among her peers. Boasts encyclopedic knowledge of arthropods that would make any hamna green with envy.
Aya Guunjoh
A Rakta girl and the star examinee of this year's incoming class. Naturally gifted in nearly every endeavor, she is eminently suited to the duties of any of the Library's twelve offices. However, there is one facet of life she finds terribly nettlesome.
Yuki Chairow
A Rakta girl who tends to go unnoticed by others. Quiet and impassive, she in fact has a secret love of prompting others to laughter. Is constantly thinking up low-key pranks to catch her peers off guard.

16 Blood Will Be Drawn When Nobles Draw Forth
RMMBBL
OH, YOU'RE GONNA SPELL IT OUT FOR ME, ARE YOU?!
THAT'S TWICE NOW YOU'VE CALLED ME A "PEASANT."
YOU ASKED HER TO REPEAT HERSELF!
SO TELL ME, YOUR HIGH-NESS...
...WHAT ROYAL LINE DO YOU HAIL FROM?!
TMP

FWISH
CLAMP
Wh...
WHOA, WHOA! THEO, OL' BUDDY!
WHAT'RE YOU DOING?
S... SOMEONE HAS TO STOP THIS!

YOU KNOW THOSE TWO?
ESPECIALLY GIVEN THAT SHE'S UP AGAINST MADHA.
SHE'S NOT ACTUALLY GONNA STAB ANYBODY. IT'LL BE FINE!
BUT SHE'S GOT A KNIFE!
ARE YOU KIDDING?! LEAVE THEM BE!
IF ANYTHING, I'D BE MORE CONCERNED ABOUT THE PERSON STICKING A KNIFE IN HER FACE.
You want some of this...?
JUST THE ONE ON THE WRONG END OF THE BLADE. MADHA AND I WENT TO THE SAME PREP SCHOOL. SHE'S A MADCAP, TRUST ME.
MADHA KAMLAN
SST...
HOW ABOUT WE FIND A PLACE TO SIT AND CHAT? JUST US GUYS!
...HUH? IT'S LIKE TRYING TO DRAG A STATUE...
TUG
TUG
SO RELAX! IT'S JUST A LITTLE POSTURING. THE LAST THING YOU WANT TO DO...
...IS TO STEP BETWEEN A COUPLE OF GIRLS WITH THEIR PAGES LOOSE.
OR TO INTERACT WITH MADHA AT ALL. IN ANY WAY. EVER.

FLICK
DRIP...
EEEK!
?!!
?!

TELL ME. WHAT DO YOU SEE?
BLOOD LIKE ANY OTHER? I IMAGINE SOME OF YOU MIGHT ANSWER AS SUCH.
THE COLOR, PERHAPS, IS THE SAME.
BUT ALL SIMILARITY ENDS THERE. WHAT YOU SEE HERE, YOU MAY NEVER POSSESS.
FOR THIS BLOOD FLOWS ONLY THROUGH THE VEINS OF THOSE NOBLE ENOUGH TO HAIL FROM HOUSE HAHAL'K.
BEFORE YOU STANDS MEDINA HAHAL'K. TAKE CARE TO REMEMBER THAT.
SHOULD YOU KNOW OF MY HOUSE, THEN THROW YOURSELF BEFORE ME NOW.
SHOULD YOU KNOW *NOT*, THEN YOU MAY FIRST PLEAD FORGIVENESS FOR YOUR IGNORANCE, AND *THEN* THROW YOURSELF BEFORE ME.
MEDINA HAHAL'K

YOU HAVE GOT TO BE KIDDING ME.
SHE'S TOTALLY RUINING MY ILLUSTRIOUS DEBUT!
あGAA
AAAHH
AND SHE KEEPS A FALCON ON HER SHOULDER? THAT'S SO UNFAIR!!
DID SHE JUST CUT HER OWN HAND TO SHOW HER BLOOD?
H-HOW... WHY IS SHE...?
Hmmmm...
SOMEONE IN THE ROOM DRAWS A KNIFE, AND SHE JUST STANDS THERE PICKING LINT FROM HER CLOTHES?
SAE FUMIS
W-WOW... CAN YOU BELIEVE IT, SAE?
WHIRL クルっ
WE HAVE TO SHARE AN INCOMING CLASS WITH TWO RUFFIANS...
IS THAT... LINT?!!
PLUCK... プチ...
PLUCK... プチ...
PLUCK... プチ...
PLUCK... プチ...

GRAB
HUH? TEPEL ?!
...UN-HAND ME.
HMPH. I APPRECI-ATE THE CONCERN...
BUT I GOT THIS.
DO YOU HAVE ANY IDEA...
THUG
FOR GOOD-NESS' SAKE!
SNUG
...
...HOW MANY DELICATE NERVE ENDINGS ARE FOUND IN A PERSON'S PALM?
YOU COULD'VE DAMAGED ONE! WHAT WOULD YOU DO THEN?!
TEPEL HURACAAN

...WONDERFUL. THIS ONE'S JUST AS ANNOYING AS MY MOTHER.
OH, FOR GOODNESS' SAKE!
UH... DO YOU ALWAYS CARRY BANDAGES WITH YOU?
AND THE CARPET! WHAT WERE YOU THINKING, LETTING YOUR BLOOD DRIP LIKE THAT?!
IT'S GOING TO LEAVE A STAIN!
PTOO! PTOO!
THAT'S ENOUGH, MADHA!
YAKO MUSUF
WHAT A LET-DOWN.
WAS IT TOO MUCH TO EXPECT A MODICUM OF REFINEMENT AMONG THE OTHER TRAINEES?
CAUICHA HOZANYK
AH, TO BE YOUNG AGAIN...
HEHE...
??????
MURMUR
MURMUR
MURMUR...
MAKE IT STOP, MAKE IT STOP, MAKE IT STOP.
TRMBL
TSITZY MIMEH
Ball of lint, ball of lint, tra la la...
DO I HAVE ANY HOPE OF STANDING OUT IN A CROWD LIKE THIS?
DO...

...
TAKE MY WORD FOR IT, THEO. YOU WANNA STAY FAR AWAY.
SETS MY HAIR ON END JUST WATCHIN ...
HUH?! YOU'RE BACK!
LOOK AT THEM.
OH, IT MAKES MY HEART GO PITTER-PAT!
PLISH
YOUNG KAFNA GRAPPLING WITH THE TRIALS OF THEIR SPRING-TIME YEARS.
ARE YOU SURE THIS IS NORMAL BEHAVIOR?
NEVER-MIND THAT! LISTEN, THEO!
I JUST GOT WIND OF SOMETHING BIG. A REAL SCOOP!
YOU DID?
IT SEEMS THAT ONE OF THIS YEAR'S TRAINEES...
...IS BEING EVALUATED AS A POTENTIAL SUCCESSOR TO THE MAGUS OF THE LIBRARY!

ALL RIGHT, SETTLE DOWN. ARE WE ALL HERE?
CLACK
CLACK
CLACK
IT'S JUST A RUMOR. I HAVEN'T LOOKED INTO IT.
I HAVEN'T THE FOG-GIEST! Not a clue!
THE MAGI CAN PASS DOWN THEIR TITLES?
A... SUCCES-SOR?
SO DON'T TAKE IT TOO SERIOUS-LIKE!
Ooh! Kafna!
IF YOU'VE YET TO CONFIRM YOUR DORMITORY ASSIGNMENT, LET US KNOW, AND WE'LL GET YOU YOUR KEY.
I'LL BE TAKING ATTENDANCE. PLEASE RESPOND WHEN YOUR NAME IS CALLED.
MURMUR
...COULD HAVE A SUCCESSOR?
THE MAGUS OF THE LIBRARY...
MURMUR...
MURMUR...
TRAINEE NUMBER 1, YAKO MUSUF!
HERE!
TRAINEE NUMBER 2...!

I'M CERTAIN I WOULD GET ALONG FINE WITH WHOMEVER.
NOT REALLY.

BETCHA BREATHED A SIGH OF RELIEF WHEN YOU FOUND OUT YOU WERE ROOMING WITH ME.

YOU'VE GOT A TELL. EVERY TIME YOU *LIE*, YOUR CHEEK TWITCHES.
WANNA KNOW SOME-THING?

...
KID-DING.
JUST

BWA-HAHA!

WHAT THE?!
WHERE DID YOU COME FROM?!
I'VE BEEN HERE...
...THE ENTIRE TIME.
YUKI CHAIROW
SHE'S SO QUIET, SHE MIGHT AS WELL BE A GHOST.
HMPH. HOW ORIGINAL. ALL THE RAKTA TRAINEES CRAMMED INTO THE SAME DORM ROOM.
SEEMS PRUDENT TO ME.
IN THE WORDS OF THE GREAT KEN KHLOE, "RACE IS NO BARRIER TO LAUGHTER, WORK, OR MEALS SHARED."
...!
"BUT WHEN IT COMES TO A PLACE TO BED DOWN, THE WISE KNOW..."
"...TO FLOCK WITH FAMILIAR FEATHER."

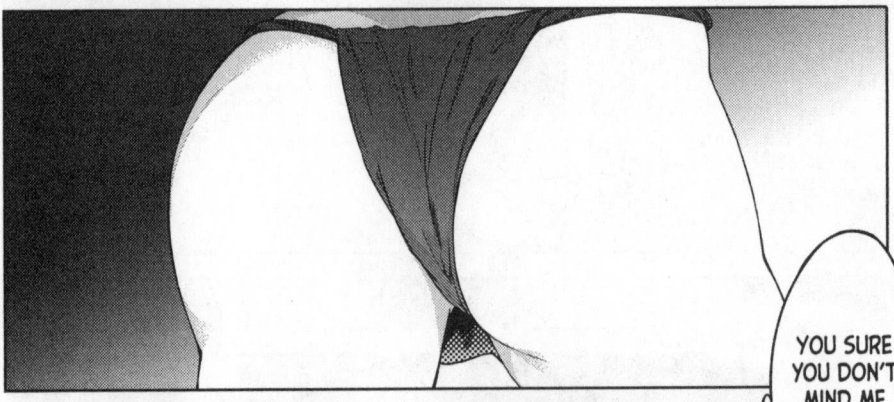

THIS IS WHAT I ALWAYS WEAR.
OH, WAIT... IS IT A LITTLE MUCH FOR HYRON SENSIBIL-ITIES?

YOU SURE YOU DON'T MIND ME TAKING THE TOP BUNK, MADHA?
IT'S FINE. BUT, UM... IS THAT GONNA BE YOUR USUAL DORM ROOM ATTIRE?
IT LOOKS A LITTLE, UH... CHILLY.

NO! IT'S FINE!

Erm...

IN FACT, I'M ON BOARD! LET'S DO THIS!
I'VE ALWAYS THOUGHT CLOTHES ARE A PAIN! I NEVER WEAR ALL THIS WHEN I'M ALONE.
FROM NOW ON, IT'S THE CREYAK WAY OR THE HIGHWAY, BABY!
ALRIGHT! THAT'S THE SPIRIT!
WANNA TRY MINE? I'VE GOT EXTRA!
AHAHA! DOES THIS EVEN COUNT AS CLOTHING ?!

FIRST IMPRESSIONS!
AFTER THAT, IT'S ALL SMOOTH SAILING!
LAY DOWN THE LAW, MIHONA.
POWER BE TO SHE WHO CLAIMS THE TOP BUNK...
...AND DELEGATES RESPONSIBILITY...
...FOR TURNING OFF THE LIGHTS AND TAKING OUT THE TRASH.
KA-CHAK
THIS IS IT! SHOWTIME!
ENTER, DEAR ROOMMATE!
IT IS I, MIHONA!
WHAT?
NGAHHH!
WHATEVER. LISTEN, TOP BUNK'S MINE.
LET'S GET SOME SLEEP.
HIT THE LIGHTS, WOULD YOU?
YES, MA'AM...

ALL RIGHT! LET'S MAKE THIS OFFICIAL.
The Hydiah
A brown-haired people residing in the Hyron Autonomous Region. Now few in number, they in fact predate the Hyron, who came about from the intermingling of the Hydiah and Jagwa.
THE NAME'S SUMOMO KAVISHMAF. PROUD HYDIAH, THROUGH AND THROUGH.
NICE TO MEET YA BOTH!
...ALV TLALOQUE.
...IS MY FRIEND UIRA.
I'M THEO FUMIS, AND THE LITTLE ONE HERE...

IT'S A PLEASURE TO BE ROOMING WITH YOU BOTH!
PSHHH! LIGHTEN UP, THEO!
WE'RE ALL BUDS, SO LET'S TALK LIKE IT!
SPEAK FOR YOURSELF.
DIDN'T YOU HEAR ME?
I SAID WE'RE *BUDS*. ***BEST*** BUDS!!
I REALLY AM HAPPY TO HAVE MADE FRIENDS SO QUICKLY, THOUGH.
WHOA, WHOA. *FRIENDS*?
HUH?! AREN'T WE?!
HMPH!
YOU TWO GO AHEAD AND PLAY BUDDY-BUDDY IF YOU WANT. BUT LEAVE ME OUT OF IT.
THERE'S NO POINT IN GETTING TOO CLOSE.
WE'VE GOT ONE SHORT YEAR TOGETHER AS TRAINEES BEFORE WE PART WAYS.
AND GIVEN HOW OFFICE ASSIGNMENTS ARE DETERMINED...
...I'D SAY WE'RE MORE RIVALS THAN FRIENDS.

HOW COULD YOU SAY THAT, ALV?!
HOW...
...!!!

...THE GIRLS HERE WILL EAT US ALIVE! WE HAVE TO BAND TOGETHER!
CL
AMP
LISTEN! IF THE THREE OF US DON'T HAVE EACH OTHER'S BACKS...
LET GO OF ME.

LET ME GUESS! *YOU* THINK THAT GIRLS WHO BECOME KAFNA ARE PRIM AND PROPER! *NICE*, EVEN!
WELL, I'VE GOT NEWS. *NICE* GIRLS DON'T PASS THE TEST. ONLY THE REAL PIECES OF WORK MAKE IT THROUGH. THE *MONSTERS*. THE *RAVENOUS BEASTS*!

GRK!
THEO!
DOES IT HAVE TO BE A COMPETITION? CAN'T WE BE FRIENDS WITH THE GIRLS, TOO?
WH ...?!
NO!

KAFNA WOMEN ARE BATTLE-HARDENED FROM CONSTANT WAR AGAINST EVERY EXPECTATION ANYONE'S EVER HAD OF THEM!
YOU WON'T FIND ANY DEMURE MAIDENS HERE! NONE OF *THESE* GIRLS ARE GONNA WALK THREE STEPS BEHIND OR OFFER QUIET NODS OF COMPLIANCE!
HOW DARE YOU?!
SOMETHING TELLS ME IT WAS LESS ABOUT PUTTING BOYS DOWN AND MORE ABOUT PUTTING YOU DOWN.
THE WAY THEY PUT BOYS DOWN, YOU'D THINK THE WHOLE WORLD WAS TURNED ON ITS HEAD!
OOH, AFTER WHAT THEY PUT ME THROUGH IN PREP SCHOOL ...!
NOW YOU'RE EXAGGERATING.
WHEN SHE GETS ANGRY, YOU CAN SEE A *SERPENT* COILED UP AT HER BACK!
ESPECIALLY MY MOM.
I'M THE YOUNGEST OF NINE. ALL GIRLS BUT ME.
MY MOM'S A KAFNA, AND TWO OF MY SISTERS, TOO.
THEY'RE AS OVERBEARING AS THE REST.
OOPS! SORRY, ALV. MY BAD.
ENOUGH GABBING. GO TO SLEEP.

THAT'S HOW I SEE IT, ANYWAY.
GUYS THAT BECOME KAFNA? THERE ISN'T A BAD APPLE IN THE BUNCH.
PUMPH
THERE'S SO MUCH I WANNA SAY TO MY NEW PALS.
I'M JUST SO RELIEVED, Y'KNOW?
OF COURSE YOU'RE GOOD GUYS. YOU HAVE TO BE!
BUT I DO!
YOU DON'T EVEN KNOW US. ME OR BLONDIE.
DUNNO WHAT MAKES YOU THINK WE'RE PALS.
YEAH, MAYBE. NO ONE WOULD PICK THIS LINE OF WORK IF THEY WANTED FAME OR FORTUNE.
Exactly!
BUT JUST FROM TALKIN' TO YOU GUYS, I CAN TELL YOU'RE BOTH DECENT PEOPLE.
BOTH THE GUYS AND THE GIRLS WHO WANT THIS LIFE HAVE TO GIVE IT EVERYTHING THEY'VE GOT.
DON'T GET ME WRONG. I THINK GIRLS WHO BECOME KAFNA ARE TRYIN' THEIR BEST, TOO.
HEHE... HE'S JUST TRYING TO BE FRIENDLY. AT LEAST, I THINK HE IS.
LAST WARNING. GO TO BED. NOT ANOTHER WORD.
I WAS JUST THINKING MAYBE YOU MIGHT LIKE TO FEEL TALL AT LEAST WHILE YOU'RE ASLEEP.
HEY! I FORGOT TO ASK. YOU WANNA SWAP FOR A TOP BUNK, ALV?

TOMORROW, WE BEGIN OUR CLASSES.
I'M GETTING SO WORKED UP THINKING ABOUT IT...
OH, NO.
I WONDER WHAT OUR DAYS IN TRAINING WILL BE LIKE.
...I DON'T KNOW IF I'LL BE ABLE TO FALL–
I'M AS NERVOUS AS I AM EXCITED.
LUCKY. I WISH I FELL ASLEEP THAT EASILY.
スゥ PFF
スゥ... PFF...
ZZZ

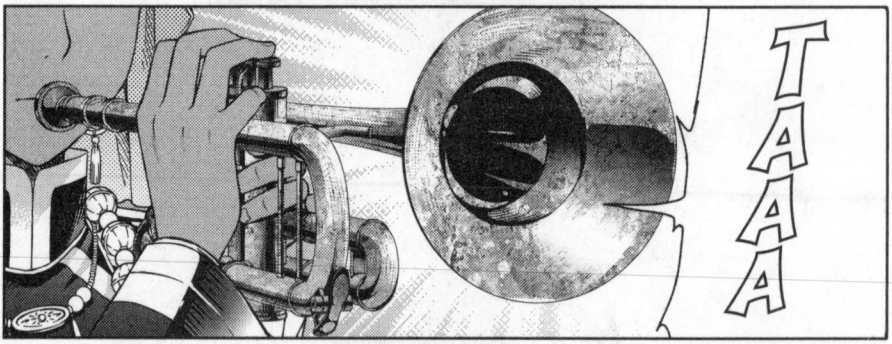
TAAA

TARARUP

TAAA

HUH? WHUH?!
TARARUP
SPRING

NRMM...

TAAA
TATATAA
TATATAA
TATATAA
TAAA
TARARUP

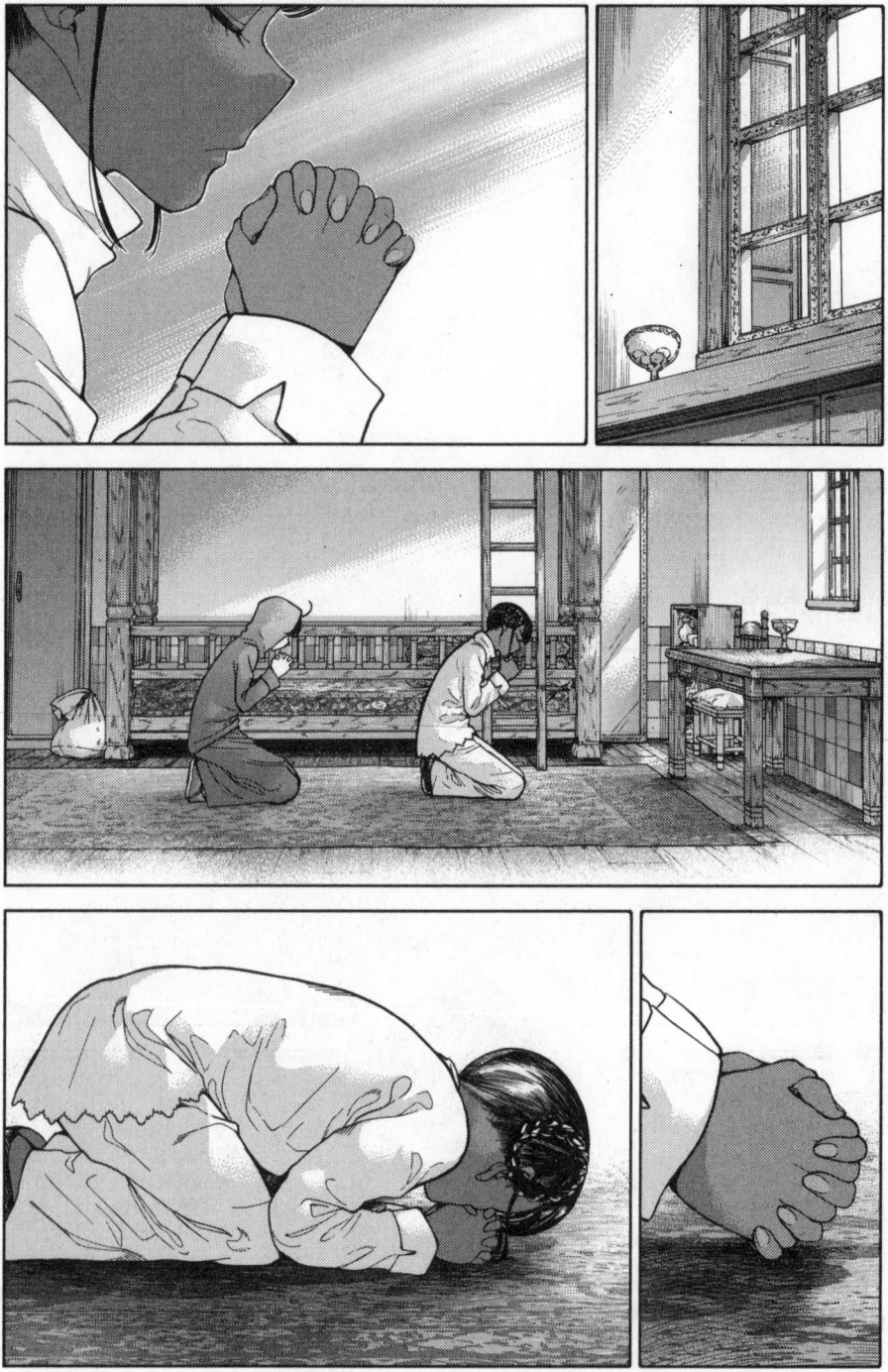

AND NOW...
...WE TURN TO THE NORTH.
NOW WE TURN.
I WAS LOOKING FORWARD TO BEING DONE WITH MORNING PRAYERS ONCE I WAS OUT ON MY OWN.
THIS IS SOOO BORING.
AND SHE'S SO PARTIC-ULAR...

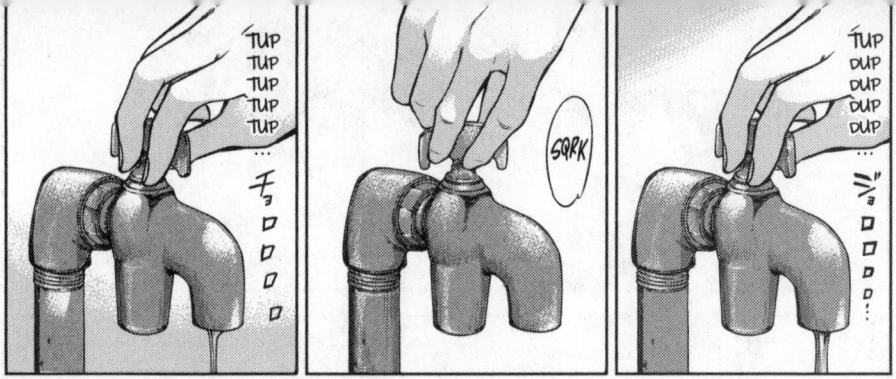
TUP TUP TUP TUP TUP ... チョロロロロ
SQRK
TUP DUP DUP DUP DUP ... ジョロロロロ...

WOOOOOW...
TUP TUP TUP TUP TUP ...

AFTZAAK MIGHT BE BLESSED WITH PLENTY OF WATER FROM LAKE TATA AND ELSE-WHERE...
...BUT IN A CITY OF OVER A MILLION, WE ALL GOTTA DO OUR PART TO MAKE SURE IT DOESN'T RUN OUT.

CAREFUL. IF YOU GET CAUGHT WASTING WATER, YOU'RE GONNA GET AN EARFUL.
SORRY. IT'S JUST SO AMAZING...

SPLSH SPLSH
VSSHHH ジャアアア

IN OTHER WORDS, DON'T DO WHAT HE'S DOING.
VSSSSS ジャアアアア
SHHA
AHHH! NOTHING LIKE A NICE, THOROUGH WASH IN THE MORNING!

Wow... How nifty...
POKE
POKE
SINCE NEITHER OF YOU ARE DOING MORNING PRAYERS, I TAKE IT WE'RE ALL MANACCHAN HERE?
I GREW UP ASIN, BUT I DON'T DO THE PRAYERS.
THEY'RE A WASTE OF TIME.
OOOOH. ALV'S A *BAD BOY!*
WHAT'S THE DEAL, THEO? NEVER SEEN A TOOTH-BRUSH?
HOW DO YOU CLEAN YOUR TEETH AFTER YOU EAT?
UM... YOU KNOW... A PIECE OF CLOTH OR A TOOTH-PICK...
YOU'RE IN LUCK. I PACKED AN EXTRA. YOU CAN HAVE MY OLD ONE IF YOU WANT!
EW. THAT IS NOT SOME-THING YOU GIVE TO SOMEONE.
REALLY? ARE YOU SURE YOU DON'T MIND?!
YOU SHOULD MIND!
ALL RIGHT! LET'S GET CHANGED AND GET OURSELVES SOME CHOW!
UM, DIDN'T THEY TELL US TO GET OUR MEASUREMENTS TAKEN FIRST?
LOOK WHO WASN'T LISTENING YESTERDAY. BIG SURPRISE.

HUH?
WH...! THEO!
HOLD UP!
WHAT'S ALL THIS MUSCLE?!
IS THIS FOR REAL?!
OH, UH... I USED TO WORK ON A MASONRY CREW.
HERE YOU ARE. YOUR TEMPORARY VESTMENTS.
THIS IS SO COOL! YOU'RE A MAN AMONG MEN!
ALV! LOOK! DID YOU SEE-
THANK YOU VERY MUCH!
UH... SOME-THING WRONG?
What's with the sour look?
THEY GAVE ME GIRLS' CLOTHES.
YES, ERM, SORRY ABOUT THAT.
They're just temporary.

WOULDN'T IT BE BETTER TO TAKE OUR MEASUREMENTS *AFTER* BREAKFAST? JUST TO BE SAFE?
I DON'T THINK IT'S GONNA MAKE THAT BIG A DIFFERENCE...
HA HA!
RISE AND SHINE!
AHA HA!
DANG, DON'T YOU FIND THIS OUTFIT DRAFTY?
HA HA!
AHA HA!
KA-CHAK
ARE YOU TWO AWAKE? IT'S TIME TO–
OOP.
EEEEEEEK!!!!

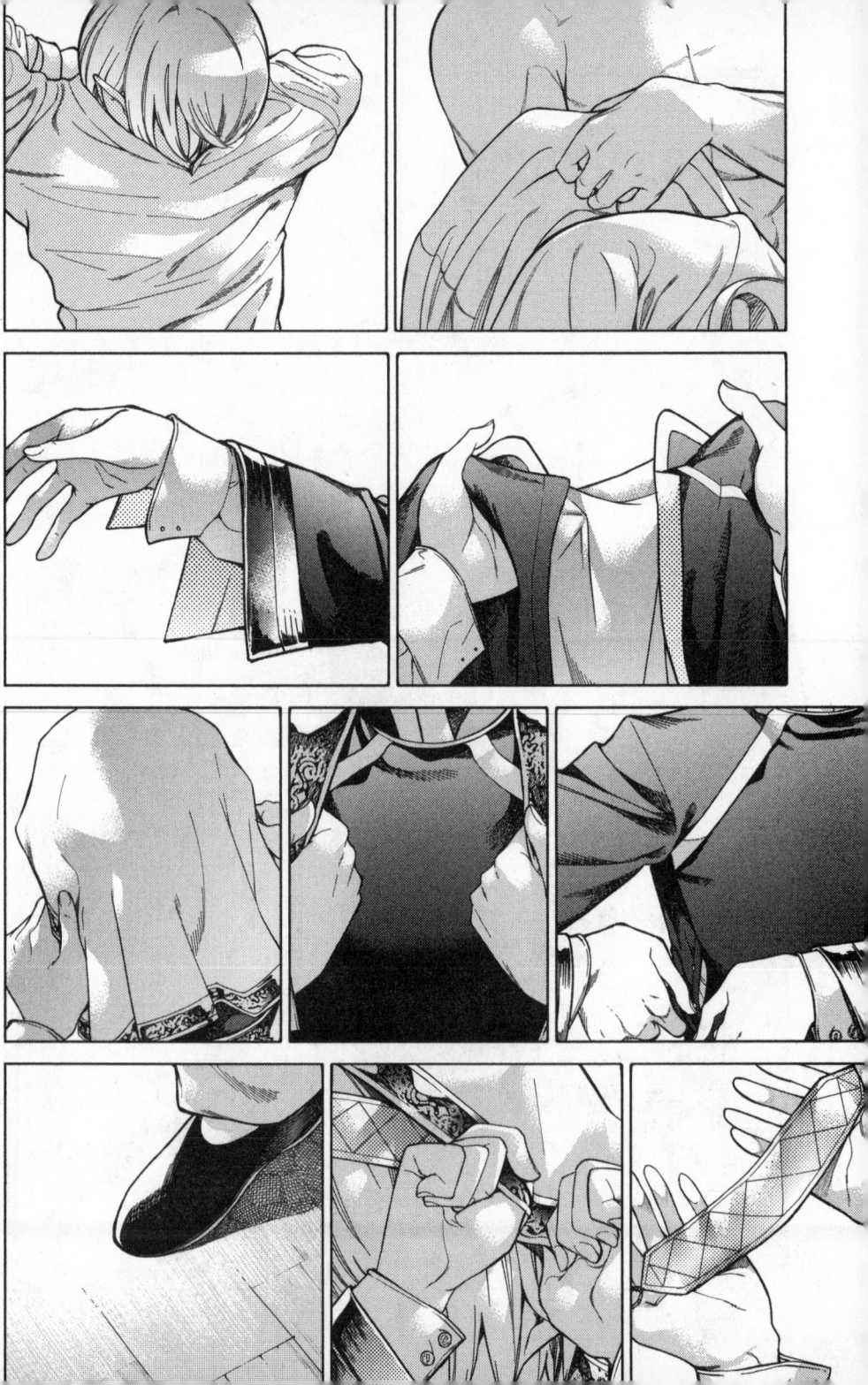

ON IT, THE SIMPLE, UNADORNED PATTERN OF A TRAINEE...

MY VERY OWN KAACHNI...

WHAT OFFICE'S CREST WILL IT BEAR AT THE END OF OUR TRAINING?

Tikeeka
Talis-mans worn about a kafna's neck.
NOT SO FAST.
WOW. I CAN'T WAIT TO PUT SOME TIKEEKA ON.
AN ITTY-BITTY TRAINEE JANGLING AROUND LIKE SOME KINDA HOTSHOT? THE OLDER KAFNA WOULDN'T LET YOU HEAR THE END OF IT!
LOOKIN' GOOD, THEO!
THANKS! SAME TO YOU TWO!
ALL RIGHT, THEN!
WHAP
THIS IS IT, MY BRETHREN!
OFF WE GO TO WAR!
OUR BATTLEFIELD? THE CENTRAL LIBRARY!
WHO PUT YOU IN CHARGE?

* KOHKWA: ANCILLARY STAFF WHO ASSIST THE KAFNA IN THEIR DUTIES.

The talented few able to surmount the grueling kafna exam won privilege to work among these walls. Their first year was spent in training, learning the arts of their new profession.

Aftzaak Library, Third Cafeteria

カチャ CLINK
カチャ CLINK
カチャ CLINK
WOBBLE... ゴト。
WOBBLE... ゴト。
OOPS. AND HERE I THOUGHT I WAS GOING LIGHT.
Of this I partake.
Look at all that!
THEY'RE GONNA THINK I'VE GOT TERRIBLE MANNERS...
ARE YOU GONNA BE ABLE TO EAT ALL THAT?
HUH...? UM, YEAH...
FOR HOW TALL YOU ARE, YOU SURE DON'T EAT MUCH.
I KNOW. IF I HAVE TOO MUCH, I GET SLEEPY.
BUT HEY! YOU GOTTA EAT MORE LIKE THEO IF YOU WANNA GROW UP BIG AND STRONG!
...
SNARF
MMM! IT'S ALL SO GOOD!
GOBBLE
CLINK CLINK
HEY! QUIT SPLASHING SAUCE ALL OVER THE PLACE!

THEO FUMIS, RIGHT?
AH, YOU MUST BE...
HEY! YOU! QUIT STANDIN' AROUND!
FIND YER SEAT AND SIDDOWN ALREADY!
SEAT'S OVER THERE. NEXT TO HER.
WOW! A SPIRIT THAT WORKS AS A KOHKWA!
HEY! HANDS OFF!
AWWW! HOW CUUUTE!
HOW 'BOUT SOME RESPECT FOR YOUR ELDERS?!

I'M THEO FUMIS. GLAD TO MAKE YOUR ACQUAINTANCE.
WOW! YOU KNOW WHO I AM ALREADY?
YOU MUST BE, UM... SAE, RIGHT?
MY LAST NAME IS FUMIS, TOO. WE MATCH!
OH! LOOKS LIKE WE'LL BE SEATMATES.
SAE! WHAT DID I TELL YOU ABOUT BOTHERING PEOPLE?!
I JUST SAID HELLO, TEPEL...
SORRY IN ADVANCE. SAE CAN BE A REAL NUISANCE.
IT'S KINDA FUNNY...
I guess we'll be sitting together!
NOD NOD
I KNOW THE PEOPLE HERE REPRESENT THE BEST OF THE BEST...
RRMMMBLL
LOOK! I CAN'T BELIEVE THOSE TWO GOT PAIRED OFF.
I KNOW! HOW IRONIC...
YAAAWN...
...BUT LOOKING AROUND, YOU MIGHT NEVER GUESS IT.

YEAH? WELL I'D HIRE A NEW EDITOR IF I WERE YOU.

YOUR *ADVICE* IS UNNECESSARY.
THERE IS NO ENTRY FOR "HUMILITY" IN THE HAHAL'K FAMILY DICTIONARY.

AS A NATIVE OF AFTZAAK, LEMME OFFER A WORD OF ADVICE.
SAVE THE TIKEEKA FOR WHEN TRAINING'S OVER.

TMP
TMP
TMP

GOOD.
IT APPEARS YOU'RE ALL PRESENT AND SEATED.

EYES UP HERE, PLEASE!

THRMP!

AS ASSISTANT SUPERVISORS ASSIGNED TO THE 86TH INCOMING CLASS OF TRAINEES, WE'D LIKE TO EXTEND OUR WELCOME.

...AS WE HELP YOU ON YOUR JOURNEY TO BECOMING UPSTANDING YOUNG KAFNA. ALL 27 OF YOU–ONE OF WHOM IS YET TO JOIN US, DUE TO SPECIAL CIRCUMSTANCES.

FOR THE NEXT YEAR, YOU WILL REMAIN IN THE CARE OF THE PERSONNEL OFFICE...

DESPITE THE LACK OF A MASK, I AM, IN FACT, KADOE.

I AM REI ANA EDAN.

TALK TO ME PLAINLY, HEAR? NO STUFFY LANGUAGE!

THE NAME'S BUSTAS D'KAYSER. I'M A CREYAK.

...NOT MUCH OLDER THAN MOST OF YOU.

HI! I'M AIKO JORAMIS, A HYRON. I'M ACTUALLY...

I KNOW. BIG SHOCK.

PUPUTO RAPUTABBIS HERE. I'M A KOKOPAH.

NOW, IF YOU'LL PLEASE REMAIN SEATED, THE HEAD SUPERVISOR SHOULD BE ARRIVING ANY MOMENT TO BEGIN CLASS.

IF YOU SHOULD HAVE ANY TROUBLES DURING YOUR TRAINING, REST ASSURED THAT WE ARE HERE TO AID YOU.

AND I AM CHISE REDD. I HAIL FROM RAKTA.

PIT

WE'VE FINISHED CARRYING THE PAPERS TO THE CLASSROOM, PROFESSOR.
VERY GOOD.

KREEK
KREEK
PAT

HEHE...
IMAGINE THE LOOKS ON THOSE POOR TRAINEES' FACES...

... OF THE *RULU OWLAI*– THE TREMOR THAT TREADS LIGHTLY.
IT WON'T BE LONG NOW BEFORE THEY'VE HAD A TASTE...

STRAIGHTEN
スクッ
!

SHHHF

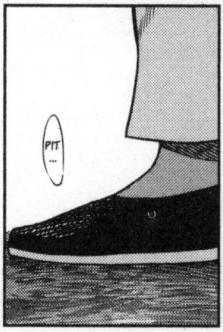
PIT
...

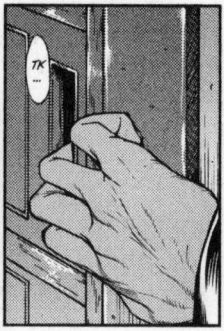
TK
...

SHHHK

SHE LOOKS, AT FIRST GLANCE...
...LIKE THE SURFACE OF A PLACID POND.

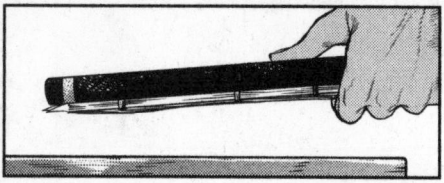

PFF...

NEITHER ECHO NOR SWIRL OF DUST STIRS IN HER WAKE.
SHFF...
EVERY ACTION IS CALM AND MEASURED.

I AM XTOH SEROS OF THE CENTRAL LIBRARY PERSONNEL OFFICE.
I WILL BE IN CHARGE OF YOUR TRAINING FOR THE DURATION OF THIS YEAR.

GOOD MORNING, PROFESSOR XTOH!

GOOD MORNING, CLASS.
I'D LIKE TO BEGIN WITH A GREETING. SHOW SOME ENTHUSIASM, PLEASE.

HRMM...
I'M AFRAID THAT WON'T DO.
COULD WE PUT A BIT MORE ENERGY INTO IT?
GOOD MORNING, PROFESSOR XTOH!
ONCE AGAIN, PLEASE.
GOOD MORNING, CLASS!
STILL MUCH TOO SOFT.
I WANT TO HEAR YOU SHOUT WITH *EVERYTHING* YOU HAVE!
GOOD MORNING, PROFESSOR XTOH!
DID YOU HEAR ME?
I SAID *EVERY-THING!*
WE'RE NOT PRE-SCHOOL-ERS.
GOOD MORNING, PROFESSOR XTOOOH!

HEAR YOU!!

I
CAN'T

KVRM
KVRM
KVRM
KVRM
KVRM
KVRM
KVRM
KVRM
KVRM
KVRM
YOUUUUUUUUUUUU...

WHEN I ASK FOR EVERYTHING YOU HAVE...
...I MEAN EVERYTHING.
I HOPE I HAVE MADE MYSELF CLEAR.
TO SUCCEED AS A TRAINEE...
...YOU WILL SPEAK WHEN I SAY SPEAK...
...STAND WHEN I SAY STAND...
...AND SILENCE YOURSELF AT MY COMMAND.
THOSE ARE THE BASICS FROM WHICH WE SHALL BEGIN.

...SHE QUAKES LIKE THE RAGING EARTH...
...AND TOWERS ON HIGH LIKE WOTAN, THE MIGHTY SPIRIT OF THE FOREST.
BUT LOOK CLOSER...
...AND YOU FIND...

TODAY'S ASSIGNMENT. TAKE ONE AND THE PASS THE REST BACK.
CONSIDER IT MY WAY OF WELCOMING YOU, AS WE EMBARK ON THE YEAR OF RIGOROUS STUDY AHEAD.
I IMAGINE YOU WEREN'T EXPECTING A TEST ON DAY ONE.
SOMETHING *LIGHT* TO WARM UP WITH.
I'VE GOT THIS!
THINK OF IT AS AN EXTENSION OF THE KAFNA EXAM.
YOUR TIME STARTS NOW. BEGIN.
PLING...

I I I N G
WH-WHAT JUST HAPPENED?
TH...
TIIING
THE WHOLE ROOM CHANGED!

PL
mmel
mmel
SHIVER

WH...?!
IT'S LIKE THEY'VE TURNED INTO...
...COMPLETELY DIFFERENT PEOPLE!

DON'T LET IT THROW YOU OFF, THEO.
YOU PASSED, TOO.
YOU MADE IT HERE JUST LIKE THEM!
GULP...
RIGHT. SO THESE ARE THE MINDS CHOSEN TO BE KAFNA.
SKRT SKRT SKRT
SKRT SKRT SKRT
SKRT SKRT SKRT
CLATTER
TSK!
IF I HADN'T TAKEN THE TIME TO RECHECK MY ANSWERS, I WOULD'VE BEEN FIRST.
TA-DAH! DONE!
CLATTER
I'M READY TO HAVE MINE CHECKED, PROFESSOR.
THAT'S ALL FOR THIS MORNING. YOU'RE FREE TO RETURN TO YOUR DORM.
SHE'S DONE ALREADY ?!
NO WAY!
CLATTER
GOOD. THIS WILL DO JUST FINE.

TIME! PENS DOWN!
THOSE OF YOU NOT FINISHED, BRING YOUR PAPERS FORWARD NOW.
LOVELY.
THREE TO DEAL WITH THIS YEAR.

DUN
DUN

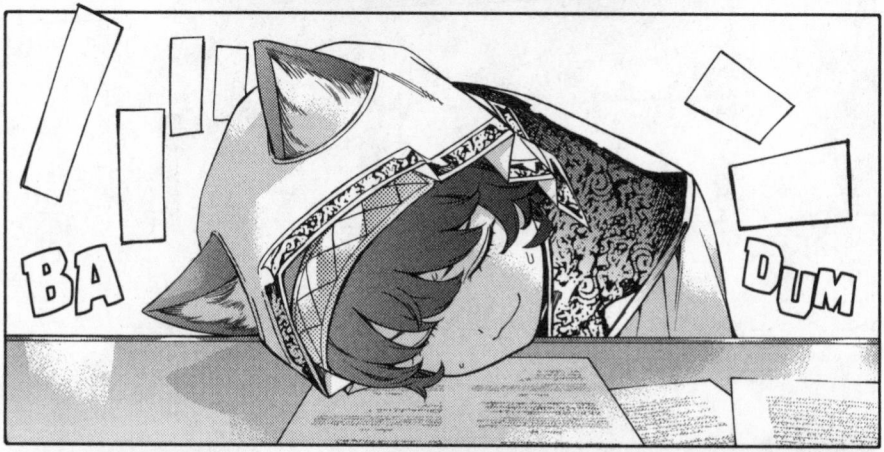
BA
DUM

PLIP
PLIP

PFFFFFFFT!
AHAHA!
AHA HAHA HAHA HAHA HAHA HAHA HAHA!
HAHA HAHA HAHA HAHA HA!!
Y...
YOU...
YOU COULDN'T EVEN FINISH?!

ALL THAT TALK ABOUT YOUR *NOBLE* PEDIGREE...
...AND YOU CAN'T EVEN MAKE IT THROUGH A PAGE OF BASIC PROBLEMS?!
MADHA! THAT'S ENOUGH!
BACK OFF, YAKO!
?!
LOOK, I KNOW THAT A JOKE AS GOOD AS THIS IS HARD TO LET PASS.
IF YOU'RE GONNA RIDICULE SOMEONE, THERE'S A *RIGHT* WAY TO DO IT.
YOU SAY YOUR PIECE ONE ON ONE, *WITHOUT* AN AUDIENCE.
BUT!

SO, HERE GOES...! HEY! WHY DON'T YOU HEAD BACK TO PREP SCHOOL?
YOU MIGHT LEARN SOMETHING THIS TIME!
NOT
ONE
MORE
WORD OUT OF YOU!!
HAH!
RIGHT ON THE MONEY.
SHALL I INTER-VENE?
WE'RE GOING, MADHA!
NO. LEAVE THEM BE.

HOW COULD ANYONE *NOT* FINISH A TEST THAT SIMPLE?
I'm serious, Blondie. I wanna know.
THIS IS MY FAULT.
IT'S 'CAUSE YOU DIDN'T GET ENOUGH SLEEP, ISN'T IT? I SHOULDN'T HAVE TALKED SO MUCH.
NO. DON'T APOLOGIZE.
THIS WAS A PERFECT DEMON-STRATION OF WHERE I'M AT.
I WAS READY FOR THIS.
I didn't even know tests could be that hard...
THE PROBLEM NOW...
...IS FIGURING OUT HOW I'M GOING TO CATCH UP.
I KNEW THIS MIGHT HAPPEN.

I MEAN, I'LL ADMIT IT WAS KINDA FUNNY SEEING HER LOSE FACE.
SHUT IT, YAKO.
WE HAVE TO *LIVE* WITH THESE PEOPLE, YOU KNOW?
YOU'VE GOT TO QUIT STIRRING UP TROUBLE.
MADHA! HEY! LISTEN TO ME!
...THAN INSULTING SOMEONE BEHIND THEIR BACK.
DON'T TALK BAD ABOUT HER WHEN SHE'S NOT AROUND. THERE'S NOTHING MORE SPINELESS...
MEANIE!!
YOU'RE LECTURING *ME*? AFTER EVERYTHING YOU'VE DONE THESE PAST TWO DAYS?! YOU... YOU...

ALL SIGNS POINT TO NO.
WHERE DO THEY GET ALL THAT *ENERGY*? THERE'S NO WAY WE'LL KEEP UP.
TZAKO NAMIR
AGE 20
(3 FAILED EXAM ATTEMPTS)
WELL, WHADDYA THINK, MADAM?
THINK WE CAN HACK IT AMONG ALL THESE YOUNGINS?
METT NANAU
AGE 19
(4 FAILED EXAM ATTEMPTS)
NOW, NOW.
IF YOU GO AROUND SAYING THAT, YOU'LL MAKE THE *REAL* FOSSIL FEEL BAD.
APPARENTLY, THE YOUNGEST IS ONLY *ELEVEN!*
THERE'S NO TWO WAYS ABOUT IT. YOU AND I ARE JUST O-L-D. A COUPLE OF FOSSILS, REALLY.
WHAT'S WORSE IS THAT MOST PASSED ON THEIR FIRST TRY.
AND THAT PROFESSOR! TALK ABOUT SCARY!

IT'S THAT TRAINEE I SAW YESTERDAY, THE ONE WHO'S SO MUCH OLDER. I THOUGHT FOR SURE THAT SHE WAS ONE OF OUR TEACHERS.
OH, UM...
Hello.
HEY, UH, NOT TO BE RUDE, BUT COULD WE ASK HOW OLD YOU ARE?
I'M 35.
THIR...?! AND YOU'RE JUST STARTING OUT *NOW*?!
WELL, I THOUGHT IT MIGHT BE FUN TO GIVE LIFE AS A KAFNA A WHIRL, SO I SAT FOR THE TEST.
I TRULY RESPECT THE LIBRARY FOR ACCEPTING ANYONE AS LONG AS THEY MANAGE A PASSING SCORE.
"GIVE IT A WHIRL" ?! Seriously ?
Do you have any idea how hard we worked to pass?!
YOU TWO MUST BE TZAKO AND METT, IF I'M NOT MISTAKEN.
HUH? HOW DO YOU KNOW OUR NAMES?
YESTERDAY'S ROLL CALL. I MEMORIZED *EVERYBODY'S* NAME. ♡
Whoa!
AND NOW THAT I'M HERE, I SUPPOSE I OUGHT TO SEIZE THE OPPORTUNITY TO BASK IN ALL THIS YOUTHFUL ENERGY!
OOPS. JUST TEASING. ♡
AHHHHH!
SHE IS SO OLD...
UNBELIEV-ABLY OLD...
I'M SORRY. I'M AFRAID I'VE HARDLY REMEMBERED ANY NAMES YET.
COULD I ASK YOURS?
WHY, I'M SOPHIE.

SOPHIE SCHWIMM.
IT'S A PLEASURE TO MEET YOU.

The Kafna in Training
The Power of a Smile
Sae Fumis
A Hydiah girl who almost never stops fidgeting. Occasionally demonstrates intense focus, able to concentrate on a single task all day long without breaks or meals. This peculiar mix of traits causes her longtime friend Tepel no small amount of grief.
Shuko Tcovach
An ordinary girl. Intelligent, cheerful, and full of energy—a wealth of wonderful traits, really, yet somehow doesn't stand out among this particular crowd.
Madha Kamlan
A spirited, somewhat boyish girl. Grew up with three sisters and nary a brother in sight, leaving her parents somewhat mystified over her confrontational nature and rough speech. Has a feminine side, too. Enjoys discussing love and romance.
Dianasys di'Ohgga
A girl with both Creyak and Hyron lineage. Though outwardly bubbly and carefree, is at heart very considerate of others, constantly watching for ways to maintain high spirits and good harmony among the group. Has the ability to sense where others fix their gaze.
Kiraha Kyamnan
A somewhat capricious girl who doesn't sweat the details—an attitude sometimes mistakenly construed by others as a lack of sincerity. But her determination shines through whenever she has a goal in mind, sending her merrily skipping along on the path to success.
Peperico Pradhatti
A Kokopah girl who is fascinated with kafna to an almost worrying extent. Worked hard to become one expressly so she'd be able to wear the signature attire. Spends her days flitting around, busily gathering new details to include in the profiles she keeps on every kafna she hears of.

The Kafna in Training
The Unyielding Majesty
Natica Quapan
A 15-year-old girl with a very lustrous forehead. Received the second best score, after Aya, on the written portion of the exam. Chose to become a kafna to support her family, as her father is ill and unable to work. A chronic worrier often heard repeating the phrase, "Just to be safe."
Medina Hahal'k
Youngest daughter of the renowned House Hahal'k. A devout practitioner of Asin—specifically the Akini denomination, known for its particularly pious adherents. Enjoys viewing artwork in her leisure time.
Sytlah Cueh
A somewhat high-strung girl who harbors no shortage of small dissatisfactions about the world. Realizes there'd be no end to her complaints if she got started, so tries not to mention them out loud. Loves the smell of ink from a newly-purchased book.
Cauicha Hozanyk
Daughter of the business magnate behind the Hozanyk Conglomerate. Has an intense distaste for ambiguity and refuses to mince words. An expert at mental arithmetic, able to instantly multiply any pair of five-digit numbers.

17 An Almost Transparent Future

...
HEH...
HEH HEH...

THESE OTHER TRAINEES, THEY'RE IN A LEAGUE OF THEIR OWN.
SHIVR
SHIVR
JUST IMAGINE, A CHANCE TO LEARN MORE ABOUT BOOKS IN COMPANY LIKE THAT.
IT'S GETTING ME ALL FIRED UP...!
FWAM
FWISH
THAT'S THE SPIRIT!
GO GET 'EM!
IT'S NO USE.

I THOUGHT MAYBE IF I SAID THE KINDA THING THE HERO IN AN ADVENTURE NOVEL MIGHT SAY, IT'D LIFT MY SPIRITS.
BUT I'M NOT FEELING FIRED UP. NOT AT ALL!
FEAR! THAT'S WHAT I'M FEELING...
WILL I END UP SLOWING THE WHOLE CLASS DOWN?!
WILL THE TEACHERS HAVE TO RETHINK THE CUR-RICULUM JUST ON ACCOUNT OF ME?
HAAAH...
I THOUGHT I MIGHT HAVE TIME TO EXPLORE THE LIBRARY WHEN I GOT HERE.
NOW I DON'T THINK I'LL HAVE TIME FOR ANYTHING!
KA-CHAK

THEO! IS EVERYTHING ALL RIGHT?
YOU CAME STRAIGHT BACK HERE AFTER LUNCH!
C'MON. YOU'RE NOT STILL HUNG UP ON THAT SILLY TEST, ARE YOU?
WHAP WHAP
IT'S NOTHING TO WORRY ABOUT! HEY, HOW ABOUT I TAKE YOU ON A TOUR OF THE LIBRARY?
I KNOW THIS PLACE LIKE THE BACK OF MY HAND!
I WAS BORN AND RAISED *INSIDE* THESE CITY WALLS, SO–
WHACK
OWWW!
LAY OFF, CHESTNUT. YOU KNOW THERE ISN'T TIME FOR A TOUR BEFORE OUR NEXT CLASS STARTS.
THAT'S ANOTHER THING! QUIT CALLING US "CHESTNUT" AND "BLONDIE"! WE'RE NOT HAIR COLORS!
CHESTNUT DOES THE JOB, SO I'M GONNA KEEP USING IT.

THE JUVENILE OFFICE IS ALSO RESPONSIBLE FOR DEVELOPING STRATEGIES TO PROMOTE READING HABITS AMONG CHILDREN.
...AND, OF COURSE, ORGANIZING AND CONDUCTING THE DAILY STORY-TELLING SESSIONS AT CENTRAL LIBRARIES TWO THROUGH FIVE.
...OTHER DUTIES INCLUDE THE SELECTION OF TITLES FOR READING WEEK...
...THOUGH I IMAGINE YOU WERE ALREADY QUITE VERSED IN THE SUBJECT.
THERE YOU HAVE IT—A BASIC LOOK AT THE FUNCTIONS OF EACH OF THE TWELVE OFFICES...
WE'D LIKE TO KNOW WHICH OFFICES YOU HAVE A PREFERENCE FOR UPON BECOMING FULL-FLEDGED KAFNA.
THANK YOU, PROFESSOR. NOW, THERE'S ONE FINAL ITEM ON TODAY'S AGENDA. A QUESTION-NAIRE.

The Twelve Offices

At a typical regional library, a single librarian might balance all manner of tasks, repairing damaged books, maintaining the catalog, and deciding upon new acquisitions as needed.

But at the Central Library, all necessary functions are split across twelve divisions. Each kafna is assigned to one, spending an entire career dedicated to its specific duties. These divisions are known simply...

...as the Twelve Offices.

- General Affairs Office
- Guidance Office
- Treasury Office
- Judicial Office
- Archival Office
- Cataloging Office
- Restorations Office
- Personnel Office
- Facilities Office
- Liaisons Office
- Juvenile Office
- Protections Office

TO BE CLEAR, WE'RE HAVING YOU FILL THIS OUT BECAUSE IT'S TRADITION...
...AND NOT BECAUSE I'LL BE TAKING IT INTO ACCOUNT.
YOUR ASSIGNED OFFICES WILL BE DETERMINED FOR YOU ACCORDING TO THE REALITIES I PERCEIVE.
MINUS, OF COURSE, THREE EXCEPTIONS.

GUIDANCE IS THE OBVIOUS CHOICE. WHY ELSE BECOME A KAFNA?
I'M DEFINITELY WRITING GENERAL AFFAIRS.
SKRT
SKRT
SKRT
SKRT

DO THEY DREAM OF WORKING IN THE COVETED GUIDANCE OFFICE?
DIRECTING OUR FUTURE IN GENERAL AFFAIRS?
IF ALL THEIR WISHES CAME TRUE, THOSE OFFICES WOULD HAVE MORE YOUNG KAFNA THAN THAN THEY COULD HANDLE.
MANAGING BUDGETS FROM THE TREASURY?

GUIDANCE! WHAT ELSE IS THERE?
SKRT
SKRT

GENERAL AFFAIRS.
SKRT
SKRT
SKRT

...THE GUIDANCE OFFICE.
SKRT
SKRT
SKRT
SKRT

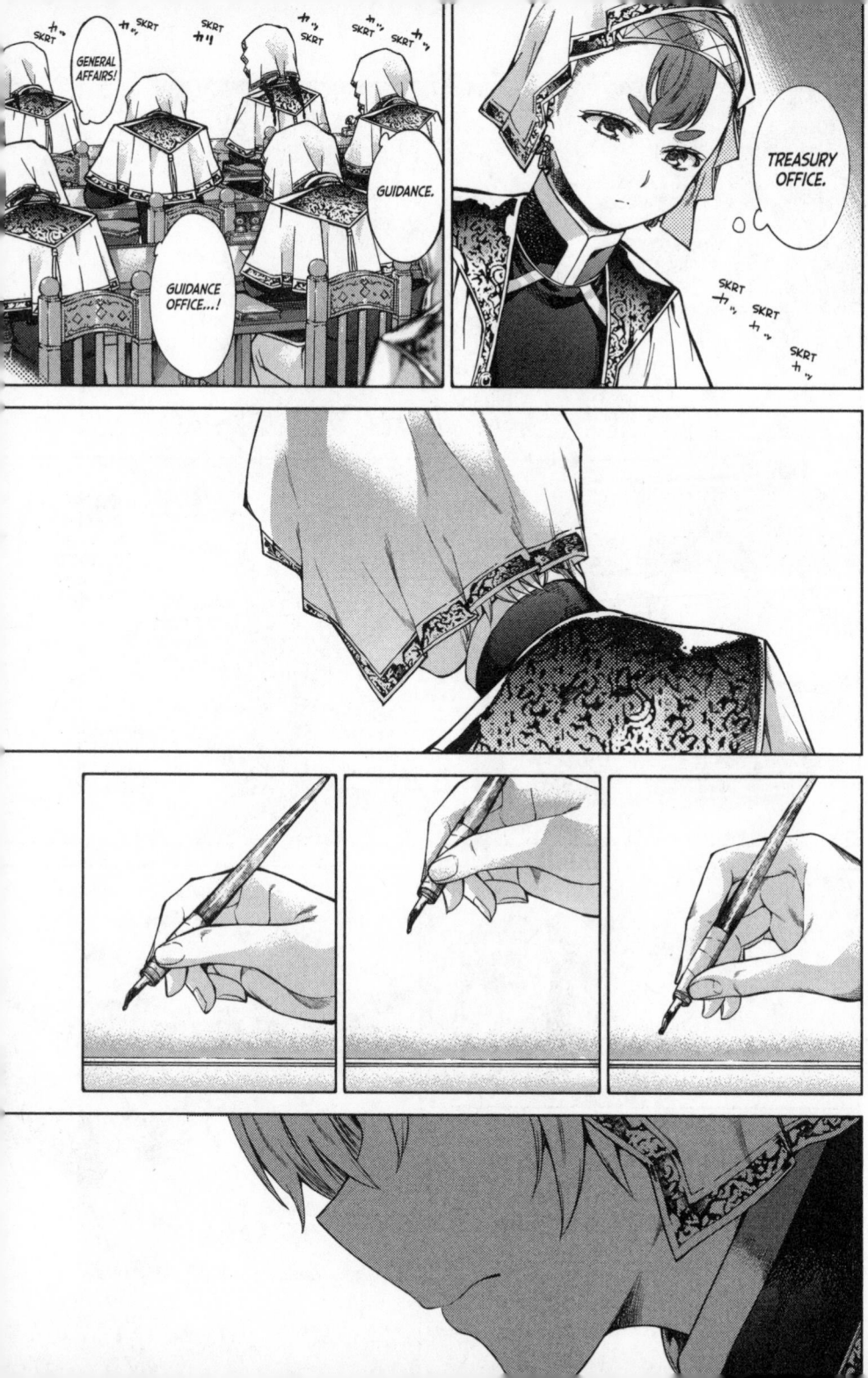
SKRT
SKRT
SKRT
SKRT
SKRT
SKRT
SKRT
SKRT
GENERAL AFFAIRS!
GUIDANCE.
GUIDANCE OFFICE...!
TREASURY OFFICE.
SKRT
SKRT
SKRT

ONCE YOUR QUESTIONNAIRE IS IN, YOU'RE FREE TO GO.
ALL RIGHT. PASS YOUR ANSWERS FORWARD, PLEASE.
CHATTER
CHATTER
BUSTLE
BUSTLE
Which did you write?
...
FLICK
FLICK
FLICK
?!
...YES, MA'AM.
MISTER FUMIS.
A WORD, PLEASE.

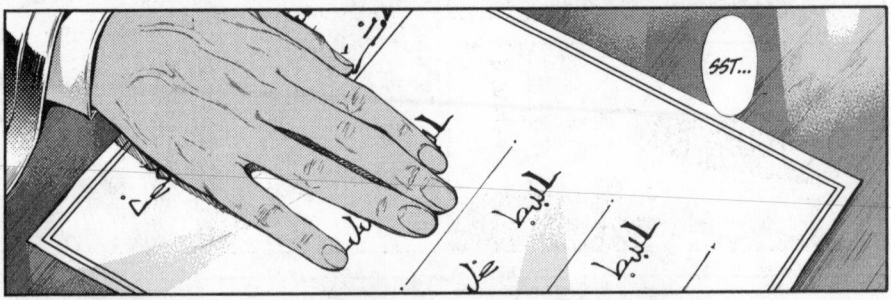
SST...

YOUR QUESTIONNAIRE IS BLANK. WHY?

ALV! THEY'RE MAKING THEO STAY BEHIND!
LET'S WAIT FOR HIM.

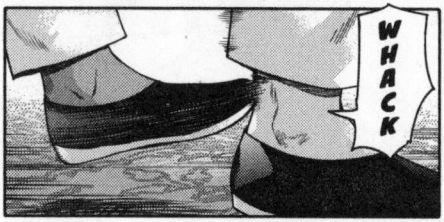
WHACK

I'M SORRY, MA'AM.
IT'S JUST THAT...
...I'M STILL NOT SURE...

YOU'RE STILL NOT SURE?

C'MON, CHESTNUT. WE'RE GOING.
IF YOU'RE GONNA KICK ME, KICK SOMETHING *COVERED!*

DO YOU MEAN TO TELL ME THAT YOU LABORED THROUGH ALL YOUR PREPARATIONS TO PASS THE EXAM WITHOUT A *SINGLE* THOUGHT...
...AS TO WHAT KIND OF ADULT YOU HOPED TO BECOME OR WHAT ROLE YOU MIGHT FILL?

HEEEY!
I BET YOU'RE FEELING UPSET ABOUT HOW THIS MORNING'S TEST WENT!

ERM, AIKO...?
IT'S NICE TO SEE HOW SHE EMPATHIZES WITH THEM, BUT I WISH SHE'D CHOOSE HER WORDS MORE CAREFULLY...

IT'S ALL RIGHT! DON'T BE SHY! MAYBE YOU'VE GOT YOUR SIGHTS SET ON THE GUIDANCE OFFICE? OR GENERAL AFFAIRS?
WRITE IT DOWN! ...ALTHOUGH, I GOTTA ADMIT, IT'S PROBABLY TRUE THAT SPOTS IN THE *POPULAR* OFFICES WILL GET SNAGGED BY THE TRAINEES WITH THE BEST GRADES.

NO. THAT'S NOT IT.

...

I...
I WANT TO DO SOMETHING FOR THE BOOKS' SAKES.
I WANT TO GIVE BACK IN THANKS FOR WHAT THEY'VE GIVEN ME.
THAT IS WHAT HAS ALWAYS MOTIVATED MY STUDIES.
BUT THE MORE I LEARN...
...THE MORE I REALIZE...
...THAT *EVERY* OFFICE IS IMPORTANT. EVERY ROLE IS NEEDED!
ALL THE OTHER TRAINEES ARE MUCH MORE TALENTED THAN ME.
IT'S HARD FOR ME TO SEE WHERE I'D FIT IN AMONG THEM.

AND THAT'S WHY...
THAT'S WHY I DON'T HAVE AN OFFICE... I DON'T HAVE A *PLACE*...
...THAT I CAN RAISE MY HEAD HIGH AND SAY *THAT'S* WHERE I WANT TO LEAVE MY MARK.

YOU DO REALIZE IT'S JUST A *SURVEY*, RIGHT? A WAY FOR US TO GET TO KNOW YOU? YOU DON'T HAVE TO MAKE SUCH A BIG *DEAL* OUT OF–

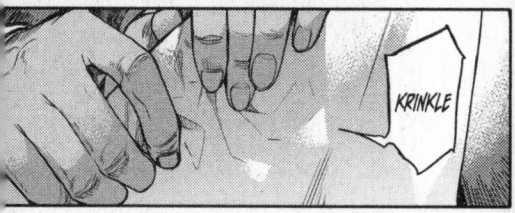

SHHHHRK
SHRK
SHRK
SHRK
SHRK

FRR
I CAN SEE...
SHH
...THIS ISN'T FOR YOU.

IN YOUR CASE, I'M SURE *ONE* CHOICE WILL BE QUITE SUFFICIENT.
DO NOT BE MISTAKEN. I AM AS INVESTED AS ANY OF YOU IN YOUR EVENTUAL ASSIGNMENTS. I OBSERVE, SEEKING TO UNDERSTAND WHERE EACH TRAINEE'S STRENGTHS LIE.
BUT THE HARSH REALITY IS THAT SUPPLY AND DEMAND FOR ANY GIVEN OFFICE RARELY ALIGN. NOT ALL TRAINEES WILL FIND SPACE IN THE OFFICE TO WHICH THEY ARE MOST SUITED.

ONLY THE TOP THREE TRAINEES...
...WILL BE GRANTED THE CHOICE OF WHICH OFFICE TO JOIN.
TO BE ABLE TO FOLLOW THE PATH OF YOUR CHOOSING...
...YOU WILL HAVE TO EARN THE *RIGHT* TO DO SO.
EARN THE RIGHT?
DO YOU MEAN...?
INDEED. OVER THE COMING YEAR...
...WE WILL BE EVALUATING YOU ACROSS ALL YOUR CLASSES, TO BE ADMINISTERED IN TURN BY EACH OF THE TWELVE OFFICES.

...!
ONLY THE TOP THREE...
ゴク
GULP...
HANG ON TO THE SLIP. WHEN YOU FINALLY HAVE YOUR ANSWER, BRING IT TO ME.
I'LL BE WAITING.

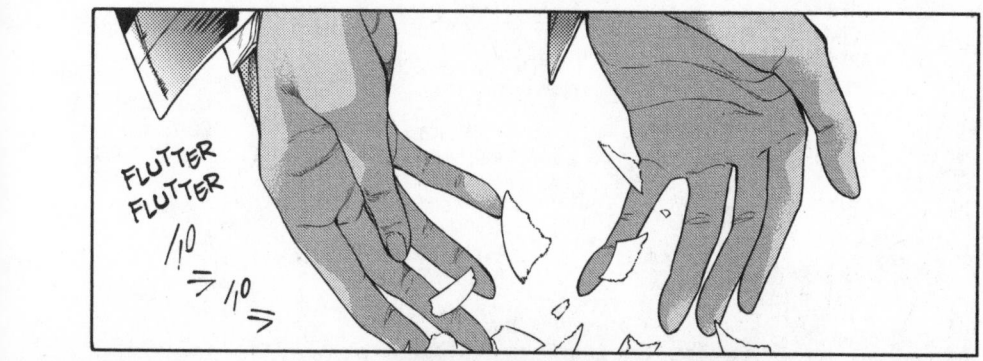
FLUTTER FLUTTER

I FEEL FOR HIM, THOUGH. AFTER BOMBING THE VERY FIRST TEST? OF COURSE HE'S GONNA BE A LITTLE SHAKEN UP.
BUT TELLING HIM TO SHOOT FOR THE TOP THREE? THAT'S JUST CRUEL.

WHOA. THAT SOUNDS INTENSE...

BUT IS THAT WHAT'S BEST FOR THEO?
HE SEEMS TO TAKE THINGS AWFULLY SERIOUSLY.

WHETHER HE SUCCEEDS OR NOT IS BESIDE THE POINT.
WHAT MATTERS IS THE *STRUGGLE*– AND OUR CHANCE TO LEARN FROM IT.
WE NEED TO LEARN AS MUCH AS WE CAN ABOUT EACH TRAINEE, SO THAT WE CAN DECIDE HOW THEY CAN BEST SERVE THE LIBRARY.

WHEN YOU SAY IT LIKE THAT, IT MAKES IT SOUND LIKE THE GIRLS ARE HERE FOR THE GLORY INSTEAD OF THE *BOOKS!*
WELL, AREN'T THEY?
IT'S A REFLECTION OF HIS PASSION.
THE BOYS TEND TO BE LIKE THAT–THEY LOVE THE BOOKS SO SINCERELY, EVERY DECISION SEEMS MONUMENTAL.
IF HE WORRIES THAT MUCH ABOUT A SIMPLE QUESTIONNAIRE, HOW'S HE GOING TO GET THROUGH THE YEAR?
I KNOW WHAT YOU MEAN. IT'S KINDA DEPRESSING BEING SURROUNDED BY SUCH AMAZING PEERS.
Y'KNOW, BACK HOME, I BELIEVED I WAS SOMETHIN' SPECIAL. A REAL PRODIGY.
I NEVER IMAGINED I'D BE COUNTING UP FROM THE *BOTTOM* OF MY CLASS.
I WAS SO CONVINCED I'D BE ABLE TO SNAG A SPOT IN THE GUIDANCE OFFICE.
MOST WILL HAVE TO MAKE PEACE WITH THE OFFICE CHOSEN FOR THEM.
THEO WON'T BE ALONE IN THIS.
SOONER OR LATER, EACH TRAINEE WILL HAVE TO STRUGGLE WITH THE PATH BEFORE THEM.
THERE *WERE* A FEW IN MY CLASS THAT HAD A HARD TIME COMING TO TERMS WITH THEIR ASSIGN-MENTS...
STILL...
I CAN'T *IMAGINE* HAVING TO WORK AMONG THE *FREAKS* IN GUIDANCE OR THE TREASURY. I'D LOSE WHATEVER CONFIDENCE I HAVE LEFT!
NOW THAT I'M HERE, I'M HAPPY WITH HOW THINGS PLAYED OUT.
NO! I DIDN'T SAY THAT!
YOU UNHAPPY HERE IN PERSONNEL?

TEEK
NOT EVERYONE CAN OBTAIN THE JOB OF THEIR DREAMS.
CHILDREN ARE QUITE MISTAKEN IN THEIR NOTIONS OF LIFE.
THEY ARE CONVINCED THAT EVERYTHING IS WITHIN REACH...
THAT THEIR VERY EXISTENCE IS ESSENTIAL TO THE WORLD.
BUT THE TRUTH IS...
...PRECIOUS FEW LIVES HAVE THE POWER TO CHANGE THE WORLD.
THEY ASSUME THEMSELVES TO POSSESS CERTAIN POWERS THAT NO ONE ELSE HAS...
...AND THAT SOMEDAY THEY WILL BE ABLE TO MANIPULATE THE HANDS OF TIME THEMSELVES, UNLOCKING A NEW AGE.

THEY'LL BE THRUST IN AMONG THE MOVEMENT, DESTINED TO LIVE OUT THEIR DAYS AS ONE AMONG COUNTLESS COGS AND SPRINGS.
MOST CHILDREN WILL NEVER SO MUCH AS BRUSH THE CLOCK FACE WITH THEIR FINGERTIPS.

MOST OF US GRUDGINGLY ACCEPT THAT TRUTH AND GO ON LIVING.
BUT ONCE IN A GREAT WHILE...

...THERE WILL BE ONE WHO STRUGGLES AGAINST IT.
TIK...

EACH CHILD REALIZES THIS TRUTH SOON ENOUGH.
THEY LEARN THE LIMITS OF THEIR ABILITIES.
THAT THEY ARE BUT A SINGLE DROP IN OUR WORLD'S SEA OF MEDIOCRITY.

HE COULD TRAVEL TO THE ENDS OF THE WORLD AND *STILL*...
...HIS FINGERS WOULD TWITCH WITH THE INCESSANT TICK THAT TELLS HIM THE HANDS ARE HIS TO TURN.

HE KNOWS. HE *FEELS* IT.

GRKK
GRKK
GRKK
...WAS JUST THE PIECE NEEDED...
AND HE FINDS THAT HIS COG, THOUGH SMALL AND SIMPLE IT MAY APPEAR...
KERSHNK
...TO CAUSE THE FROZEN HANDS OF THE AGES TO TURN ONCE MORE.
THNK
TH-THNK

YOU MAY THINK THESE WORDS GRANDIOSE.
BUT I URGE YOU TO GIVE THOUGHT TO THE POSSIBILITY...
...THAT A TINY PART OF SEEING IT TO FRUIT COULD REST HERE IN OUR OWN HANDS.

WOW! BEING A TEACHER IS A BIG RESPONSI-BILITY!
YEAH. AND STARTING THIS YEAR, IT'S *YOUR* RESPONSIBILITY, TOO.
You know that, right?

WE WILL BE WATCHING YOU, DEAR STUDENTS.
AND WE EXPECT YOU TO STRUGGLE AND SUFFER!!

BEFORE THIS YEAR IS THROUGH...
...I'LL FIND THE OFFICE TO WHICH I'M MEANT TO DEDICATE MY LIFE.
AND I'LL WIN THE RIGHT TO CHOOSE IT WITH MY OWN TWO HANDS!
I'VE MADE UP MY MIND.
SHOW US WHAT YOU CAN DO, THEO FUMIS!

THE WALL BEFORE ME IS HIGH.

BUT I HAVE NO CHOICE BUT TO SCALE IT!

HERE I COME!
THEO FUMIS IS PLAYING TO WIN!

YOU'RE BACK!
WHAT WAS ALL THAT? DID SOMETHING HAPPEN?
Is everything all right?
YEAH? WHAT'S THE STORY?!
...
HEH, HEH.
I GUESS YOU COULD SAY THAT.
MY *NAME* IS THEO, THANK YOU VERY MUCH!
Hmph!
HEH!
WELL, WHAT DO YOU KNOW?
SEEMS BLONDIE'S OVER HIS SLUMP.
...!

NOW I REALLY AM FIRED UP!
TELL YA WHAT, ONCE YOU START FINISHING TESTS WITHIN THE TIME LIMIT...
...THEN I'LL START CALLING YOU BY YOUR ACTUAL NAME.
HEY, UM... ALV?
REMEMBER HOW I FINISHED MY TEST IN TIME?
OH, FOR CRYING OUT LOUD...
FINE. SUMOMO. HAPPY?
THIS IS IT.

The Kafna in Training
The Harried Handlers
Mihona Qoahau
A girl who just can't seem to nail the critical moments. Easily swayed by whatever novel she's currently reading, and endlessly dreams of playing the suave, sophisticated heroine—a dream that never quite works out. Tends to choke, so her results don't reflect her true talent. Feels more harried than ever looking after herself as a kafna in training.
Yako Musuf
A girl who has it all together and is very sensitive to others' feelings. Dislikes any hint of turbulence among the group. At prep school, was the one to mend relations whenever her seatmate Madha—a neverending source of turbulence—stirred up trouble. Feels more harried than ever looking after Madha as a kafna in training.
Tepel Huracaan
A girl who has it all together but is quick to chide others for their shortcomings. At school, was the one to drag her longtime friend Sae back to her seat whenever the latter began wandering the room during class. Feels more harried than ever looking after Sae as a kafna in training.

The Kafna in Training
The Ends of the Spectrum
Mett Nanau
An ambitious young woman whose persistence and enthusiasm carried her through to success despite four failed exam attempts. Nineteen years old and loves to discuss politics.
Sophie Schwimm
The oldest in this class of trainees, at just 35 years old. Lazy by nature. Puts her perpetually unkempt hair up in braids each morning, but lately, even that seems like far too much trouble. A mother of one, she lives by the motto that everything always works out in the end.
Tzako Namir
A somewhat pessimistic young woman who has trouble seeing her own strengths. Failed the kafna exam three times yet found herself unable to stop trying, ultimately passing on attempt number four. Twenty years old and very self-conscious of how much younger the other trainees are.
Tutull Xiu
The youngest in this class of trainees, at just 11 years old. Loves reading—an earnest, simple love that carried this prodigy straight into life as a kafna. Consumes new books at an astounding pace, yet takes time to savor the novels that she loves.

18
Acting the High and Mighty Regal Curatrix
HOOT
HOOT
HOOT
HOOT

THIS ISN'T IT, EITHER...
NO... NOT THIS ONE...
SHOULD I TRY THE MAIN LIBRARY?
NO...
HOW WOULD I EVEN BEGIN TO EXPLAIN...?

ALL RIGHT, EVERYONE!
IT'S TIME FOR BED!

TOMORROW'S YOUR BIG MATRICULATION CEREMONY.
YES, MA'AM!
I WANT TO SEE YOU BRIGHT-EYED AND BUSHY-TAILED IN THE MORNING.
GOOD NIGHT, MA'AM!

IF YOU'D LIKE, I'LL BE HAPPY TO TRACK IT DOWN FOR YOU.
Here or in the main com-plex!
I TOOK THE GUIDANCE CLASSES, TOO, YOU KNOW, BACK WHEN I WAS A TRAINEE.

OH! HELLO THERE, THEO.
SEARCHING FOR A BOOK?

...
UM...

NO! I'M FINE! THANK YOU, THOUGH!
GOOD NIGHT, PROFESSOR EDAN!

SNXXX...
グオー
クカー
SIZZRK...

PFF...
ブゥ
PFF...
ブゥ

Recorded in these pages was the story of a girl and the world she witnessed.

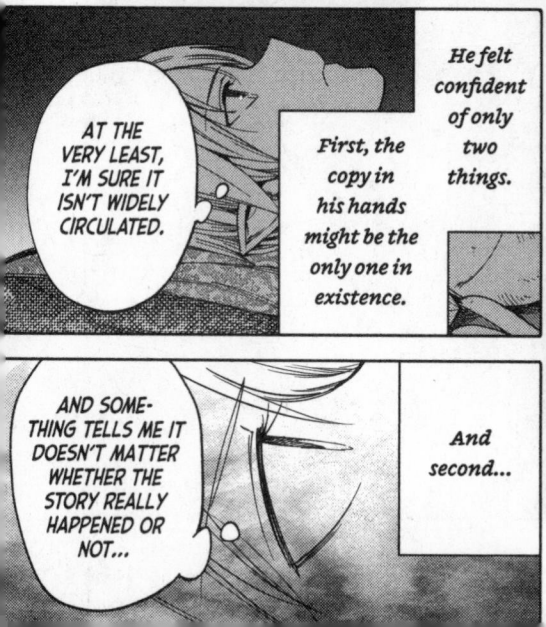
AT THE VERY LEAST, I'M SURE IT ISN'T WIDELY CIRCULATED.
First, the copy in his hands might be the only one in existence.
He felt confident of only two things.
AND SOMETHING TELLS ME IT DOESN'T MATTER WHETHER THE STORY REALLY HAPPENED OR NOT...
And second...

For years now, Theo had wrestled with whether to accept its words as truth...
...as he was well aware of what tragedies could occur when people are swayed by falsehoods dressed up as facts.

...that what was written on its pages...
...had the power to destroy the very world in which he lived.

PULL IT TOGETHER, SAE! DON'T YOU DARE YAWN DURING THE CEREMONY!
YAAAWN... I'M SOOO SLEEEEPY...
GASP!!
Just beyond the library's primary complex rested its "first" in another sense.
...were its most recent additions. Many times had the grounds and facilities been expanded.
AFTZAAK LIBRARY, MAIN COMPLEX
AFTZAAK MUSEUM OF ART
AFTZAAK MUSEUM OF HISTORY
In truth, the Central Library's three main structures...

Bacab Castle, General Headquarters to the Continental Libraries. This was the site to which Komako Kaulikk, with the aid of the Royal House of Koora...

...had ferried texts from across the continent to ensure their safety during the Great War of the Races. It was in this castle that the Central Library began.

TMP
TMP
TMP
TMP
WOOOW...
HEY. LOOK.
I BET THOSE ARE THE NEW KOHKWA THIS YEAR.

Unlike the kafna, each was employed by a specific office from the outset—the Twelve had leave to post hiring notices as necessary.
The kohkwa carried out orders of the kafna, assisting the librarians in their duties.
DID YOU FORGET TO PACK YOUR SENSE OF TACT WHEN YOU LEFT HOME?
LUCKY. LOOK AT HOW MANY MORE GUYS THEY HAVE.
I WANNA BE A KOHKWA.
THAT'S THE BLOND KID WHO SHARED THE ENCYCLOPEDIAS WITH ME. LOOKS LIKE HE PASSED...
And their ranks...
...included no small number of boys who had tried but failed to become kafna.
...and mercenaries helping to fulfill the duties of the Protections Office.
Makeup of the kohkwa was varied, from those hired to carry out unskilled labor, to craftsmen assisting the Restorations Office...
MURMUR
MURMUR
MURMUR
MURMUR

LOOK! OVER THERE!!
WHOA!
...!
ペコッ BOW

WOW. JUST LOOK AT 'EM ALL.
PLISH
EVERYONE'S IN ATTENDANCE, FROM US NOBODY TRAINEES ALL THE WAY UP TO THE BIG KAFNA WHO CALL THE SHOTS!
THAT'S RIGHT.
I MAY STILL BE JUST A TRAINEE...
...BUT I'M PART OF THIS NOW! I'M ONE OF THE PROTECTORS OF BOOKS!
MURMUR
MURMUR
MURMUR
MURMUR
THEO'S HERE. HE PASSED BY JUST NOW...

FAR BE IT FROM ME TO BEGRUDGE YOU A FAVOR, BUT I HAVE TO ADMIT, AS I FLEW HIM OVER...
...HE SEEMED LIKE ANY ORDINARY BOY. MINUS HIS APPEARANCE, THAT IS.
...SEDONA.
I CAN'T IMAGINE WHAT IT IS YOU EXPECT OF HIM.
HE HAS LITTLE NEED OF MY PALTRY EXPEC-TATIONS.
THEO'S BEING FAR EXCEEDS MY POWERS OF IMAGINATION.
HOW HARD HE TOILED FROM HIS TENDER YEARS TO BE HERE TODAY, I DO NOT KNOW.
EXPECTA-TIONS?
FROM ME? PERISH THE THOUGHT.
MUR MUR
MUR MUR
MUR MUR

WE GO THROUGH THIS EVERY YEAR.
AFTER ALL THESE DECADES, ONE WOULD THINK YOU'D HAVE GOTTEN USED TO IT BY NOW.

HAAAH...
MY TUMMY HURTS.

GET BACK HERE!
ZIP!
MAYBE I OUGHT TO GO REFRESH MYSELF.

...
AND I WON'T. I HATE SPEAKING IN FRONT OF AN AUDIENCE.
BUT I HAVEN'T.

"ESTEEMED LADIES"?
...BUT I MUST WONDER HOW APPROPRIATE IT IS FOR TWO ESTEEMED LADIES TO DISCUSS DELICATE MATTERS SO AUDIBLY.

NOT TO INTRUDE, MASTER TAKSHA...

THE CEREMONY IS ABOUT TO BEGIN!
THIS IS NOT THE TIME TO POTTER ON THE POTTY! YOU'LL JUST HAVE TO HOLD IT IN!
IT'LL ONLY TAKE A MOMENT! I'LL BE IN AND OUT IN A JIFFY!

LUCKY FOR YOU, I'M GLAD YOU'RE HERE.
YOU HAVE MY WORD.
I have my own duties to attend to today.
SEE THAT MASTER KOMAKO STAYS SAFE, WOULD YOU?
KEEP ME SAFE? PAH!
SHRF
IT HAS BEEN FAR TOO LONG.
GREETINGS, K'AHKUM.
HEAVENS. COULD YOU DISPENSE WITH THAT "MASTER" NONSENSE?
PLEASE FORGIVE ME FOR NOT CALLING UPON YOU MORE OFTEN SINCE MY BEING NAMED A SAGE.
PAH.
YOU KNOW VERY WELL HOW I FEEL ABOUT GETTING INVOLVED IN THE LIBRARY'S INTERNAL POLITICS.
KEEPING COZY WITH THE STEWARD OF PROTECTIONS WOULDN'T SET MUCH OF AN EXAMPLE, NOW WOULD IT?

KTAK

SHP

MURMUR...
MURMUR...
MURMUR...

I AM PLEASED TO ANNOUNCE...
...THAT THE PLENUM FOR THE NEW YEAR IS NOW IN SESSION.
HRMPH. HERE WE GO...
WE'LL BEGIN WITH THE STATE OF THE LIBRARY...

AH. I'D BEEN MEANIN' TO TELL YA.
I RAN INTO THAT FRIEND OF YOURS. THE ONE YOU TOLD ME ABOUT. YOU KNOW, THE LITTLE ONE WITH THE EARS.

I KNEW IT!
THE SYNTHSPIRIT'S ASSAULT! IT *WAS* THEO FUMIS AND YOU TOGETHER THAT DAY!

...BUT WITH MANA LIKE THAT, THERE WASN'T MUCH NEED FOR CHANCE.
I SUPPOSE I WAS LEFT ITCHIN' TO KNOW MORE. I SET OUT FOR A STROLL, HOPING I MIGHT CHANCE ACROSS HIM...
THE EXAM INTERVIEW. THAT WAS THE FIRST TIME.
BUT PLEASE TELL ME, HOW DID YOU MEET?
And who said anything about a synthespirit's assault?
WHAT DO YOU MEAN YOU "KNEW IT"?
PARDON ME. I MEANT SIMPLY, "HOW INTERESTING"...
I CAN'T SAY WHETHER THAT'S A GOOD OR BAD THING, THOUGH.
...ALONG WITH A NEW GROUP OF KOHKWA NUMBERING...
AND THIS YEAR, WE WELCOME TO OUR RANKS 27 NEW KAFNA...
I SEE WHAT YOU WERE SAYING. THERE IS INDEED SOMETHING ABOUT HIM.
IF THE WAY THE BOY AND I MET WERE IN A NOVEL, I'D PUT IT BACK ON THE SHELF. PLOT'S TOO CONVENIENT.
NOTHING IS MORE EXCITING THAN A STORY WITH AN ENSEMBLE CAST, WITH THAT CLIMACTIC SCENE WHEN THE PROTAGONISTS FINALLY MEET!
YOU SEEM QUITE PLEASED TO HEAR IT.
I AM.
YOU NEED NOT PRETEND.
SINCE THE DAY THE EMISSARY WAS SEALED AWAY, NOT A MOMENT HAS PASSED IN WHICH YOU HAVEN'T DAZZLED THE IMAGINATION.
NOW, IF YOU'LL EXCUSE ME, I HAVE TO GO ACT HIGH AND MIGHTY FOR A TICK.
THAT IS MY JOB, AFTER ALL.
AND WITHOUT FURTHER ADO...
...A WORD FROM THE LIBRARY'S GENERAL REPRESENTATIVE, OUR VERY OWN KOMAKO KAULIKK!
HRMPH.

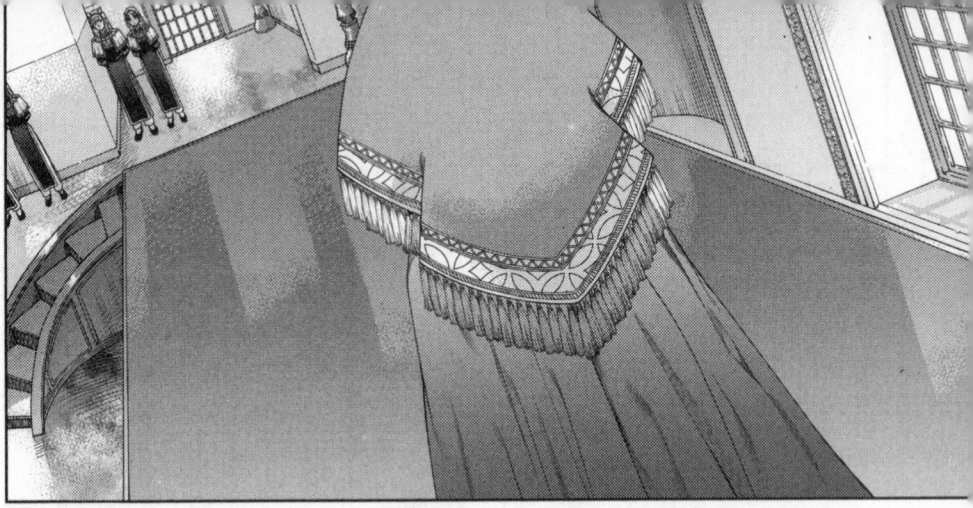

WHSPR WHSPR
HAVE YOU HEARD?
MASTER KOMAKO WAS ONLY *THIRTEEN YEARS OLD* WHEN SHE DEFEATED THE CALAMITY!

SHRP

SHP
...!
...

An artifact able to carry a speaker's voice by amplifying its vibrations via sky mana.
A phonos-taff—

...

TAKE IT AND GO.
I'VE NO NEED FOR BAUBLES.
FFFT...
PEOPLE OF THE LIBRARY!
SOME OF YOU HAVE HEARD IT BEFORE...
...OTHERS OF YOU SHALL HEAR IT FOR THE FIRST TIME.
BUT I ASK THAT YOU *ALL* TAKE IT FIRMLY TO HEART.
RMBL
I'LL NOT BORE YOU WITH AN OLD WOMAN'S RAMBLINGS.
THERE IS BUT ONE THING I HAVE TO SAY.
JOLT

WE ARE NOT...

...THE HAND OF JUSTICE.

THERE ARE MANY IN THIS WORLD WHO SEEK TO DISMANTLE THIS LIBRARY.
IT IS TRUE THAT A LARGE NUMBER OF THE TEXTS WE WATCH OVER WERE ONCE PRIZED POSSESSIONS OF OTHERS.
IN THAT SENSE, ARE WE NOT A FORCE OF EVIL, HOARDING FOR OURSELVES OBJECTS OTHERS HOLD DEAR?
PERHAPS THEY ARE THE ONES WHO ARE JUST, AND IT IS WE WHO ARE IN THE WRONG.
INSOMUCH AS WE ARE THE GUARDIANS OF TEXTS...
...SO TOO ARE WE THEIR TYRANTS. WE MUST NOT PUSH THAT TRUTH FROM OUR MINDS.
TOO MUCH CONFIDENCE IN ONE'S OWN RIGHTEOUSNESS...
...SEEDS JUSTIFICATIONS...
...FOR BLINDLY STRAYING FROM THOSE SELFSAME IDEALS.
TOO MANY ATROCITIES AMONG HISTORY'S PAGES HAVE BEEN WROUGHT...
...BY THOSE CLAIMING TO MARCH UNDER THE BANNER OF JUSTICE!
SO SEAR THESE WORDS IN YOUR HEARTS AND MINDS!
WE HAVE BUT ONE CALLING!
WE ARE GUARDIANS, NOT RULERS!

THE LIBRARY EXISTS FOR ONE PURPOSE ALONE!
WE PROTECT TEXTS!

YOOM
CLAP
CLAP
CLAP
CLAP
THAT IS ALL.
I PRAY FOR YOUR SUCCESS IN ALL YOUR ENDEAVORS.
AND NOW...
THANK YOU VERY MUCH, MASTER KOMAKO.
...A WORD FROM THE TWELVE SAGES IN RESIDENCE, ALL OF WHOM ARE CONTINUING THEIR TERMS OF SERVICE INTO THE NEW YEAR.
FWRSH
REPRESENTING IS MASTER TAKSHA, STEWARD OF THE GENERAL AFFAIRS OFFICE.

KLAK
KLAK
SHF...
HIEA
STEWARDS!
STEP FORWARD!
KLAK

THRMP

OH, GOLLY GEE!
IT'S MASTER PIARA! TO THINK I'M SEEING THE PRIDE OF MY PEOPLE WITH MY VERY OWN TWO EYES!
SHE'S SO COOL! TOO COOL!
AND SO RIS-QUÉ ...!
THAT'S MASTER SEDONA ON THE FAR LEFT!
Look! Look!
MEOW!
THE MOST POWERFUL MAGUS IN THE LIBRARY! NO! IN THE WHOLE WORLD!
SO THAT'S SEDONA BLEU, HUH? I WONDER WHO'S REALLY IN CHARGE.
MASTER SEDONA, OR THE THREE HEADS OF THE ACADEMY?
WOW! STEWARD OF THE PROTECTIONS OFFICE!
FRIENDS AND COL-LEAGUES!
IT IS WITH GREAT HONOR THAT WE STAND BEFORE YOU TODAY!
AS STEWARD OF THE LIBRARY'S OFFICE OF...

I HAD NO IDEA SEDONA WAS SUCH AN IMPORTANT PERSON!
CLAP
CLAP
CLAP
CLAP
CLAP
THANK YOU! AND NEXT UP...

WOOOW!

MUFMUF...
CHATTER CHATTER

SHE LOOKED SO COOL UP THERE! WHAT A SPEECH!
...BUT EVERYTHING AFTER THAT ONE MOMENT IS A BLUR.
I KNEW IT! I TOLD YOU GUUNJOH WAS GONNA REPRESENT THE TRAINEES!
I KNOW A LOT OF OTHER STUFF MUST HAVE HAPPENED DURING THE PLENUM...
YOU LOVE TALKING POLITICS, DON'T YOU?
IT'S RUMORED THAT THERE'S AN UNSPOKEN RULE THAT ALL LANDED RACES HAVE TO BE REPRESENTED AMONG THE SAGES, AND...

MUFMU
THAT'S POWER DYNAMICS AT PLAY RIGHT THERE!
DID YOU SEE?! BOTH THE GUIDANCE OFFICE AND THE TREASURY OFFICE ARE LED BY RAKTA!
BUSTLE BUSTLE

CAN A TRAINEE JUST WALK IN AND ASK FOR A MEETING WITH ONE OF THE STEWARDS?
HOW AM I SUPPOSED TO RETURN SEDONA'S BOOK NOW?
GASP...
FWISH...
HE'S
HE'S

THEO?!
Where are you going?
SORRY! I HAVE TO GET THROUGH!
HEY! WHAT'RE YOU-?!

WOULD THE KIND OF PERSON WHO BECOMES A STEWARD...
...EVEN REMEMBER A LITTLE BOY LIKE ME FROM A VILLAGE FAR AWAY...?
WHY DID SEDONA LEND IT TO ME?
I NEED TO KNOW IF I OWN THE ONLY COPY OF THAT BOOK!
TMP
THERE'S NO ONE HERE.
BUT THIS SURE DOESN'T LOOK LIKE AN EXIT TO THE OUTSIDE...
WHY THE DOWNCAST EYES?
MAYBE THAT BREEZE...
...WAS JUST MY IMAGINATION.

GREETINGS, THEO FUMIS.
I WAS BEGINNING TO WONDER IF YOU'D EVER ARRIVE.

The Kafna in Training
The Markedly Conspicuous
Cynthea Loh Tei
The 27th trainee of this incoming class. A girl yet to be revealed for reasons that will eventually become clear.
Patee Catl
Daughter of the esteemed House Catl. Calm and gentle in nature, but bafflingly uninformed about the world in general. Often oblivious to matters outside the purview of the kafna exam—even things others might deem common sense.
Sala Sei Sohn
A Kadoe girl who is fascinated with magi to an almost worrying extent. Quite curious about the relationship between mana and people, and is often seen conducting her own individual investigations on the subject. Tends to talk nonstop when she gets excited, a quality for which she was endlessly scolded by her parents.
Tsitzy Mimeh
A girl with a morbid fear of social interaction. Didn't take to cooking, laundry, or sewing, but has always loved to write. The strokes of her pen are blindingly swift, and the letterforms left behind are so immaculate and uniform, one might assume they came from type on a press bed.

The Kafna in Training
The Guiding Hands
Rei Ana Edan
A 32-year-old Kadoe. Has two children of mixed heritage with her Hyron husband. Enjoys baking sweets in her free time.
Bustas d'Kayser
A 25-year-old Creyak who is in love with falling in love. Quickly develops crushes on kohkwa, but is slow to act, instead analyzing the potential relationship to pieces, after which she determines there's no common ground to be had and moves on to the next crush. Skilled at cooking and handicrafts.
Chise Redd
A 43-year-old Rakta woman and the deputy head supervisor for the current class of trainees. An expert swordfighter as well as a kafna, and qualified as an instructor at the swordfighting academy run by her family. Immensely strict with herself; with others, strict but fair.
Puputo Raputabbis
A 29-year-old Kokopah and the only male supervisor for the trainees this year. Perpetually bears a sullen expression, and is thus easily misconstrued as being in a sour mood—a fact that bothers him a little, as that's just how his face naturally rests!
Xtoh Seros
A 58-year-old Hyron and the head supervisor responsible for the education of the current batch of trainees. Feared by some for her reputation as the rulu owlai—the tremor that treads lightly. Silent and delicate at times; ferociously intimidating at others.
Aiko Joramis
A 17-year-old Hyron who easily gets along with anyone regardless of gender or age, but who is superbly unsubtle. Can't take a hint, and is the perpetrator of many an awkward silence. A source of grief for the other supervisors, as three days after being lectured, she's back to doing whatever warranted a lecture in the first place.

"CONSIDER YOUR LOAN RENEWED."
19 Reunion at Aftzaak
"AS LONG AS YOU CONTINUE TO LOVE BOOKS..."
"...I AM SURE WE'LL MEET AGAIN."

Y-YES! IT HAS!
IT'S SO GOOD TO SEE YOU AGAIN...
...SE-

MUCH TIME HAS PASSED...
...HASN'T IT, THEO?

NO NEED FOR "MASTER" WHEN IT'S JUST THE TWO OF US.
BUT KEEP THAT BETWEEN YOU AND ME, HM?

HMPH!
I MEAN, UM... MASTER SEDONA.

TELL ME, SHINJI...
ASSISTANT STEWARDS OF THE PROTECTIONS OFFICE
MISAKI VERTE
SHINJI VERTE
SHALL WE TAKE A WALK OUTSIDE?
TELL ME, HOW FARES YOUR SISTER?
SHE'S WELL, THANK YOU!
YOU JUST DON'T GET IT, DO YOU?
YOU KNOW WHAT MASTER SEDONA WOULD SAY?
WHY GO TO THE TROUBLE OF LEAPING UP TO THE GALLERY JUST TO JUMP BACK DOWN AGAIN?
YES! CALLING DOWN FROM ON HIGH BEFORE LEAPING TO GROUND LEVEL IS THE WHOLE POINT!
OF COURSE, MASTER SEDONA WOULD LOOK COOL DOING ANY-THING.
HMMM, WHATEVER.
FWSHHH
"WHAT KIND OF A FATEFUL REUNION IS IT...
...IF YOU HAVEN'T GONE TO THE TROUBLE OF MAKING IT COOL?!"
AND SO ON.
UH-HUH. AND THE FACT THAT YOU'RE UP HIGH MAKES IT COOL?

YOU KNOW...
...EVERYTHING CHANGED FOR ME AFTER THAT DAY.
YOU AND THE OTHER KAFNA...
...YOU'RE THE WHOLE REASON I'M STANDING HERE NOW!
I...
...I DON'T THINK I COULD EVER THANK YOU ENOUGH!

MY ACTIONS WERE HARDLY OF NOTE.
I MAY HAVE GIVEN YOU A GENTLE PUSH FROM BEHIND, BUT I HAVE NO RECOLLECTION LEADING YOU HERE BY THE HAND.
YOU GOT HERE ON YOUR OWN, ON YOUR OWN STRENGTH.
YOURS...
...AND YOUR SISTERS'...
...AND THAT OF THE PEOPLE YOU'VE RALLIED AROUND YOU IN LIFE.
OH! BEFORE I FORGET!

THE BOOK YOU LENT ME! I BROUGHT IT WITH ME!
IT'S BACK IN MY DORM ROOM. I'LL BRING IT BY TOMORROW...
...SO IF YOU COULD JUST LET ME KNOW WHERE TO...
....
...
TELL ME, WHAT DID YOU THINK OF IT?
HOW DID IT MAKE YOU FEEL?

IT'S... A LOT TO TAKE IN.
TOO MUCH, REALLY...
THERE WASN'T ANY-ONE...
...I MEAN... NOT EVEN MY SISTER... I COULDN'T TALK WITH ANYBODY ABOUT THE THINGS I READ INSIDE...
WHY DID YOU GIVE IT TO ME? HOW COULD YOU LEAVE...
...A BOOK LIKE THAT...
...IN MY HANDS? I WAS YOUNG AND POOR, IN A VILLAGE FAR FROM ANYTHING.
THAT BOOK-
FWSHHH

THE THINGS THAT BOOK SAYS ARE DANGEROUS!
IF IT FELL INTO THE WRONG HANDS...
...THAT BOOK COULD RIP APART THE SOCIETY EVERYONE WORKED SO DESPERATELY TO BUILD!

I SEE I WAS NOT WRONG TO PLACE IT IN YOUR HANDS.

I DID NOT ENTRUST THAT BOOK TO YOU WITH ANY PARTICULAR INTENT OR EXPECTATION IN MIND.
THEO, THERE IS ONE THING I WOULD ASK YOU TO BELIEVE.

TO BE HONEST, I LONG FOR ALL THE WORLD TO KNOW ITS PAGES.
I AM SURE YOU UNDER-STAND, SUCH A DREAM WILL NEVER BE REALIZED.

I SIMPLY WISHED FOR YOU TO READ IT.

YOU WERE ABLE TO UNDERSTAND ITS WORDS FOR WHAT THEY ARE.
ERM!
NO! I, UH...
...IT'S NOT LIKE I BECAME A KAFNA WITH SOME GRANDIOSE DREAMS OR ANYTHING!
I...
AND YOU CHOSE TO WALK THE KAFNA PATH.
I CANNOT EXPRESS WHAT GREAT DELIGHT THAT BRINGS ME.
I JUST ...
DID IT 'CAUSE I LIKE BOOKS, AND...
...AND BECAUSE...
HOW IS IT?
YOUR NEW LIFE AS A KAFNA, I MEAN.
...EVERYTHING ABOUT YOU WAS SO AWE-INSPIRING.

IT'S EVEN HARDER THAN I IMAGINED.
THE OTHER TRAINEES ARE ALL SO TALENTED.
I'M ALREADY HAVING TROUBLE KEEPING UP WITH THEM.
IT...
...MAKES ME TREMBLE A LITTLE, THINKING ABOUT IT...
...BUT...

I AM SURE THAT IT IS THE TREMBLING...
...OF A WARRIOR AS HE GOES TO BATTLE!
IT SEEMS...
...YOU'VE GROWN WELL BEYOND THE NEED FOR GENTLE PUSHES ON THE BACK.
SQK...
I'M AFRAID I MUST BE GOING, THEO.
IT BRINGS ME MUCH JOY THAT OUR PATHS HAVE CROSSED AGAIN.

WAIT!
THE BOOK! HOW SHOULD I GET IT BACK TO Y-
KEEP IT.
HUH?!
TELL ME, THEO.
WHAT DO YOU PICTURE WHEN YOU HEAR THE WORD "FATE"?
DO YOU IMAGINE A FORCE THAT TRANSCENDS HUMAN COMPREHEN-SION?
DO YOU IMAGINE A DESTINY WE EACH CARRY FROM BIRTH?
DO YOU IMAGINE IT AS A WARRIOR BEING ORDERED TO VANQUISH A DARK LORD WITH A SWORD THAT ONLY HE CAN REMOVE FROM THE STONE?
OR PERHAPS AS A BEAUTIFUL MAIDEN THAT FALLS FROM THE SKY AND PROVES TO BE YOUR TRUE LOVE?

THE MANNER IN WHICH THAT BOOK CAME TO YOU...
...COULD PERHAPS BE WAVED AWAY AS HAPPENSTANCE, A FEW FICKLE WHIMS COMPOUNDED BY A MOMENT OF FORGETFULNESS.
SURELY IT IS FAR TOO MUNDANE AN OCCURRENCE FOR A GRANDIOSE LABEL LIKE "FATE," YES?
BUT HERE IS WHAT I PERCEIVE.
I SEE A DASH OF CAPRICE, MIXED WITH...
...A SINGLE KIND GESTURE...
...AND AN UNFORESEEN MISTAKE.
ALL FLAVORED WITH THE PINCH OF COURAGE YOU MUSTERED TODAY.
THE ENCOUNTERS THAT MIGHT CHANGE OUR LIVES ARE IN FACT NEVER FAR FROM HAND.
THAT IS WHY I CHOOSE TO SAVOR THE TINIEST EVENTS OF MY MOST ORDINARY DAYS.
IN FACT...
...I TAKE GREAT PRIDE IN THAT APPROACH TO LIFE.
AND I AM CERTAIN NOW MORE THAN EVER–

IT WAS FATE THAT LET CROSS OUR PATHS!

BUT...
...SEDONA, PLEASE WAIT...!
WHAT ABOUT...
PAUSE...
I...
...I MEAN...
PLEASE, KEEP THE BOOK.
I AM CERTAIN THAT SOMEDAY, SOMEHOW, YOU WILL FIND IT OF USE.

A PART OF ME HOPED...
...WOULD INCLUDE WORDS TO THAT EFFECT.
THE PROTECTIONS OFFICE, THEO. WE'LL BE WAITING FOR YOU.
...THAT THIS REUNION...
THEY WOULD NEVER TAKE FROM ME...
BUT I SHOULD KNOW BETTER.
...THE BURDEN, THE PAIN, THE JOY OF MAKING THAT DECISION FOR MYSELF.
OF COURSE SEDONA WOULDN'T SAY ANYTHING LIKE THAT.
I MUST CAREFULLY TURN EACH ONE.
IN THE BOOK THAT IS THE STORY OF MY LIFE, THE PAGES TO COME WILL BE THE HEAVIEST.
I AM CERTAIN THAT JUST BEYOND THE ANGUISH...

...I WILL FIND A RELEASE OF THE MOST SUBLIME KIND.
I WILL VISIT YOU AGAIN.
ONCE I CAN CALL MYSELF A TRUE KAFNA.
I EAGERLY AWAIT THE DAY.

Thus once more...

...crossed two who held the fate of the world in their hands...

One of them,
a champion
destined to
protect the
world...

The other,
a force of
darkness
destined
to tear it
asunder.

The reunion long promised had finally arrived.

To be continued.

Young characters and steampunk setting, like *Howl's Moving Castle* and *Battle Angel Alita*

KC
KODANSHA
COMICS

Beyond the Clouds © 2018 Nicke / Ki-oon

A boy with a talent for machines and a mysterious girl whose wings he's fixed will take you beyond the clouds! In the tradition of the high-flying, resonant adventure stories of Studio Ghibli comes a gorgeous tale about the longing of young hearts for adventure and friendship!

The adorable new odd-couple cat comedy manga from the creator of the beloved *Chi's Sweet Home*, in full color!

Praise for *Chi's Sweet Home*

"Nearly impossible to turn away... a true all-ages title that anyone, young or old, cat lover or not, will enjoy. The stories will bring a smile to your face and warm your heart."

—School Library Journal

Sue & Tai-chan

Konami Kanata

Sue is an aging housecat who's looking forward to living out her life in peace... but her plans change when the mischievous black tomcat Tai-chan enters the picture! Hey! Sue never signed up to be a catsitter! *Sue & Tai-chan* is the latest from the reigning meow-narch of cute kitty comics, Konami Kanata.

Sue & Tai-chan © Konami Kanata/Kodansha Ltd.

KC KODANSHA COMICS

CUTE ANIMALS AND LIFE LESSONS, PERFECT FOR ASPIRING PET VETS OF ALL AGES!

For an 11-year-old, Yuzu has a lot on her plate. When her mom gets sick and has to be hospitalized, Yuzu goes to live with her uncle who runs the local veterinary clinic. Yuzu's always been scared of animals, but she tries to help out. Through all the tough moments in her life, Yuzu realizes that she can help make things all right with a little help from her animal pals, peers, and kind grown-ups.

Every new patient is a furry friend in the making!

SAINT ☆ YOUNG MEN

A LONG AWAITED ARRIVAL IN PREMIUM 2-IN-1 HARDCOVER

After centuries of hard work, Jesus and Buddha take a break from their heavenly duties to relax among the people of Japan, and their adventures in this lighthearted buddy comedy are sure to bring mirth and merriment to all!

Saint Young Men © Hikaru Nakamura/Kodansha L

The art-deco cyberpunk classic from the creators of *xxxHOLiC* and *Cardcaptor Sakura*!

"Starred Review. This experimental sci-fi work from CLAMP reads like a romantic version of *AKIRA*."
—Publishers Weekly

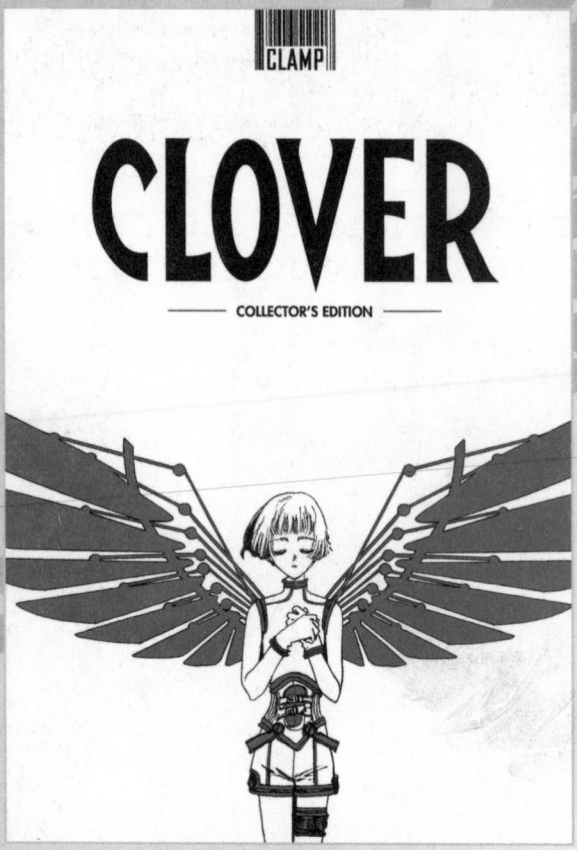

CLOVER © CLAMP·ShigatsuTsuitachi CO.,LTD./Kodansha Ltd.

Su was born into a bleak future, where the government keeps tight control over children with magical powers—codenamed "Clovers." With Su being the only "four-leaf" Clover in the world, she has been kept isolated nearly her whole life. Can ex-military agent Kazuhiko deliver her to the happiness she seeks? Experience the complete series in this hardcover edition, which also includes over twenty pages of ravishing color art!

KC
KODANSHA COMICS

MAGIC KNIGHT RAYEARTH

25TH ANNIVERSARY EDITION

CLAMP

A BELOVED CLASSIC MAKES ITS STUNNING RETURN IN THIS GORGEOUS, LIMITED EDITION BOX SET!

This tale of three Tokyo teenagers who cross through a magical portal and become the champions of another world is a modern manga classic. The box set includes three volumes of manga covering the entire first series of *Magic Knight Rayearth*, plus the series's super-rare full-color art book companion, all printed at a larger size than ever before on premium paper, featuring a newly-revised translation and lettering, and exquisite foil-stamped covers. A strictly limited edition, this will be gone in a flash!

KC KODANSHA COMICS

Magic Knight Rayearth 25th Anniversary Manga Box Set 1 © CLAMP-ShigatsuTsuitachi CO.,LTD./Kodansha Ltd.

The beloved characters from *Cardcaptor Sakura* return in a brand new, reimagined fantasy adventure!

"[*Tsubasa*] takes readers on a fantastic ride that only gets more exhilarating with each successive chapter." —Anime News Network

In the Kingdom of Clow, an archaeological dig unleashes an incredible power, causing Princess Sakura to lose her memories. To save her, her childhood friend Syaoran must follow the orders of the Dimension Witch and travel alongside Kurogane, an unrivaled warrior; Fai, a powerful magician; and Mokona, a curiously strange creature, to retrieve Sakura's dispersed memories!

Tsubasa Omnibus © CLAMP © CLAMP-ShigatsuTsuitachi CO.,LTD./Kodansha Ltd.

Tsubasa: WoRLD CHRoNiCLE © CLAMP-ShigatsuTsuitachi CO.,LTD./Kodansha Ltd.

"Clever, sassy, and original....*xxxHOLiC* has the inherent hallmarks of a runaway hit."
—NewType magazine

Beautifully seductive artwork and uniquely Japanese depictions of the supernatural will hypnotize CLAMP fans!

xxxHOLiC OMNIBUS 1

CLAMP

xxxHOLiC © CLAMP-ShigatsuTsuitachi CO.,LTD./Kodansha Ltd.
xxxHOLiC Rei © CLAMP-ShigatsuTsuitachi CO.,LTD./Kodansha Ltd.

Kimihiro Watanuki is haunted by visions of ghosts and spirits. He seeks help from a mysterious woman named Yuko, who claims she can help. However, Watanuki must work for Yuko in order to pay for her aid. Soon Watanuki finds himself employed in Yuko's shop, where he sees things and meets customers that are stranger than anything he could have ever imagined.

KC KODANSHA COMICS

Magus of the Library 4 is a work of fiction. Names, characters, places, and incidents are the products of the author's imagination or are used fictitiously. Any resemblance to actual events, locales, or persons, living or dead, is entirely coincidental.

A Kodansha Comics Trade Paperback Original
Magus of the Library 4 copyright © 2020 Mitsu Izumi
English translation copyright © 2020 Mitsu Izumi

All rights reserved.

Published in the United States by Kodansha Comics, an imprint of Kodansha USA Publishing, LLC, New York.

Publication rights for this English edition arranged through Kodansha Ltd., Tokyo.

First published in Japan in 2020 by Kodansha Ltd., Tokyo as *Toshokan no daimajutsushi*, volume 4.

ISBN 978-1-63236-916-1

Printed in Canada.

www.kodanshacomics.com

9 8 7 6 5 4 3 2
Translation: Stephen Kohler
Lettering: Paige Pumphrey
Editing: Ryan Holmberg
Kodansha Comics edition cover design by Phil Balsman

Publisher: Kiichiro Sugawara

Director of publishing services: Ben Applegate
Associate director of operations: Stephen Pakula
Publishing services managing editor: Noelle Webster
Assistant production manager: Emi Lotto, Angela Zurlo